BACKPACK
FLY
FISHING

BACKPACK FLY FISHING

A Back-to-Basics Approach

DANIEL E. STEERE

Skyhorse Publishing

Skyhorse Publishing books may be purchased in bulk at special discounts for sales promotion, corporate gifts, fund-raising, or educational purposes. Special editions can also be created to specifications. For details, contact the Special Sales Department, Skyhorse Publishing, 307 West 36th Street, 11th Floor, New York, NY 10018 or info@skyhorsepublishing.com.

Skyhorse® and Skyhorse Publishing® are registered trademarks of Skyhorse Publishing, Inc.®, a Delaware corporation.

Visit our website at www.skyhorsepublishing.com.

10 9 8 7 6 5 4 3 2 1

Library of Congress Cataloging-in-Publication Data is available on file.

Cover design by Tom Lau
Cover photo credit: Zach Steere

Print ISBN: 978-1-63450-749-3
Ebook ISBN: 978-1-63450-750-9

Printed in China

Contents

Foreword *by* Tom Oliver   vii

Author's Note   xi

Introduction   xiii

1   SIMPLIFLY! THE RATIONALE FOR BACKPACK FLY FISHING   1

2   ASCAL IN ACTION: THE BACKPACK FLY FISHING PROCESS   15

3   WHAT'S THE CATCH: THE FISH AND WHERE
AND HOW THEY LIVE   31

4   TRAVELING LIGHT: EQUIPMENT YOU WILL AND
WILL NOT NEED   59

5   IT WORKS! EXAMPLES OF BACKPACK FLY FISHING
IN ACTION   83

6   OH, AND BY THE WAY: ADDITIONAL CONSIDERATIONS
AND CONCERNS   141

Afterword: A Different Way of Thinking   167

Appendix: Accessibility and Access for People with Disabilities   173

Acknowledgments   177

For Further Reading   179

Photo Credits   185

Foreword

Bats flutter and swoop, etching wild patterns across the sky on their nocturnal patrol. Slight ripples dimple the water's otherwise serene surface in intermittent pools surrounded by clusters of lily pads. Dusk stealthily approaches. Suddenly a large splash to my left awakens me from the previous enchantment of the evening. I reflexively swivel my head to catch what my startled imagination insists must be a monster fish. Instead, it is my fellow fisherman and good friend Dan Steere who has just fallen into the lake on his first-ever fly-fishing trip. In his defense, it's very difficult to keep your footing on the bases of the lily pads while fly casting. And even though he swears to his wife, Kathy, later that night that he would never fish again, he returns to White City Lake in central New Jersey to catch many fish, including his personal best calico bass.

Since those early days, Dan has gone on to fish the white fly hatch on the Housatonic River in western Connecticut, the Chéticamp River in Nova Scotia for salmon, Point Judith Pond in Rhode Island for stripers, a small farm pond in northern New Jersey using a hare worm fly to catch largemouth bass, and many other streams and lakes throughout New England, New Jersey, Pennsylvania, and Montana—among many others.

One adventure worth noting occurred on Yellowstone Lake while camping in Yellowstone National Park with his family. While fishing on the lake, Dan noticed what appeared to be trout hitting the surface of the water. Attempting to catch the fish using dry flies proved unproductive. Analyzing the situation, Dan switched to a hare's ear nymph—determining that the trout were actually going for emerging flies (nymphs swimming to the surface to hatch). Dan's attention to detail and fisherman's intuition resulted in a few fine cutthroat trout.

In Dan's book, *Backpack Fly Fishing*, you will discover Dan's acumen for catching fish in many different environments and situations. Through his descriptions of the various fish he catches, he demonstrates his appreciation for the beauty of each and every species of fish. His writings include many insightful and down-to-earth approaches to backpack fly fishing. You will be fascinated with his keen awareness of nature and its intricacies, his simple and pure love of fishing, and the personal elements with which he infuses his narrative.

Hopefully Dan's book on backpack fly fishing will entice you into a new way of thinking about fishing in a more simplified, enjoyable manner. As you read this book, his enthusiasm will rub off on you and lure you into this simplified approach to fly fishing. He has shared many of his memorable experiences using creativity and deductive reasoning to outsmart fish in many circumstances and under a wide variety of conditions. After reading *Backpack Fly Fishing*, you will certainly be well on your way to acquiring the same skills and techniques that Dan has spent so many years diligently developing.

Tom Oliver, Crosswicks, New Jersey

Tobyhanna Creek, Pennsylvania.

Author's Note

Because both men and women can enjoy backpack fly fishing and the strategies described in this book, I have elected to use the general term "flyfishers", as opposed to the more cumbersome terms "flyfishermen and -fisherwomen".

Much of the information contained in this book is the cumulative result of over thirty years of fishing, often with flyfishers who were more skilled and knowledgeable than I am. I wish I could remember whom to credit for each tidbit of knowledge, but I do not. Suffice it to say that I thank them all for sharing their fishing wisdom and company with me. I have, however, indicated in the text whenever I have drawn information from specific published sources.

All fish photographed in this book were released unharmed.

Introduction

Backpack fly fishing is perhaps the most consistently enjoyable form of fishing for a wide range of people. Its appeal is simple: a fly rod, a backpack with some simple equipment, and a desire to explore. Preparation for a fishing trip is minimal, and often an opportunity to fish is a secondary by-product of another fun outdoor activity. And, most importantly, it can be as effective as other strategies in terms of catching a wide range of fun and challenging fish on a fly rod.

My preference for backpack fly fishing evolved over a number of years. I came to fishing later in life (in my late twenties), so initially everything was new and interesting to me. I started with spin fishing (which I still do), but when my dad brought home a first edition of Zane Grey's *Tales of Freshwater Fishing* from our local library sale with its period photographs of Zane and his brothers fishing with those strange long rods with the reels at the very end, I was immediately drawn to the idea of fly fishing. I talked about it incessantly, enough so that my wife Kathy bought me my first fly rod in February in anticipation of my April birthday. (I guess she just didn't want to hear me talk about it anymore. . . .) And so began my love affair with fly fishing and fly rods. With my friend Tom Oliver's guidance, I started on bluegills, with one memorable crappie on my second outing. At that point I owned one fly rod and one box of flies, carried in an old Pendleton flannel shirt. My dad gave me my first fly-tying kit, and I learned to tie my own flies through discovery and by following Dick Stewart's *Universal Fly Tying Guide*. From there, I ventured into trout fishing. My fly rods accumulated, as did the fly boxes filled with flies in my vest. Then, I discovered bass fly fishing after reading Dave Whitlock's groundbreaking book on the subject and Dick Stewart's bass fly-tying book. I added specialized heavier fly rods to my collection, and I continued to fly fish and tie flies.

But, as with many hobbies, I discovered that more is not necessarily better. I missed the early days of my first fly rod and my first fly box. I came to realize that my favorite places to fish were out of the way streams and ponds

A woodland stream along a hiking trail.

that you hike into and where nature, and not other flyfishers, surrounds you. And I also came to realize that I was happiest when hiking, camping, bird-watching, and fishing with other people, particularly my family.

So, I started to focus on the minimal essential equipment that could fit into my backpack. I started leaving the waders and vest at home. When going someplace, I would simply grab my backpack and take it with me. Often, I would not even open it for fishing, but many times I would, and I caught fish in the way that I like best.

This book was written to introduce you to this fun, relaxing, and effective approach to fly fishing. You will benefit from reading this book if you are . . .

- a flyfisher who wants to try a simpler, less encumbered, more relaxed approach to the sport;
- an outdoors person who likes to hike, camp, bird-watch, and so forth, and who would like to start fly fishing in order to extend your appreciation of the outdoors;
- someone who mostly spin fishes with lures or bait and who would like to fly fish also but without the commitment to full and expensive fly-fishing gear;
- a serious hiker who would like to be prepared to fish when you encounter secluded or seductive waters that you may never pass again in your travels.

If any of these describe you, then I am confident that you will learn and benefit from reading the strategies and tactics described in this book. Mostly, you'll have some fun!

Chapter One

Simplifly!
The Rationale for Backpack Fly Fishing

Picture yourself:

You're hiking through the woods with friends or family, maybe doing some bird-watching or tree or wildflower identification. It's a beautiful day, and you stop occasionally to drink some water, eat some trail mix, and enjoy the peace of the deep woods. As you continue on your hike, you first hear and then come across a small stream with miniature plunge pools and long riffles. You're not sure if it has a name, but you do suspect that it could hold some fish. You quickly assemble your backpack fly rod, tie on a small caddis imitation (say, a size 18 Henryville Special), and make a short cast into the largest pool. A wild, 6-inch brook trout rises to your fly. . . .

You're staying at a bed-and-breakfast for a three-day getaway for you and your significant other. There is a rack of brochures of nearby attractions in the front hall of the inn, and you pick up one about a local state park. As you

McIntosh Brook, Nova Scotia.

read the brochure and study the map of the park, you see that a small pond can be accessed by a trail, and the brochure informs you that the lakes and ponds of the park hold warmwater fish such as bass, bluegills, and crappies. You get up early the next day, make the bumpy drive to the trailhead, and hike a mile and a half with your backpack and fly rod. Mist is rising off of the pond when you get there, and you hear occasional splashes of fish hitting insects or amphibians off the surface. You see a beaver lodge at the far end of the pond, and you see a bass leap clear of the water and turn a complete cartwheel while chasing a dragonfly. You rig up on your rod with a cork

A bluegill feeds on the surface of a small pond.

popper and make several casts to open areas next to thick stands of lily pads, making sure to retrieve the popper slowly as its legs twitch seductively. On your seventh cast, a fish takes your popper and, with a deep bend in your rod, you fight it as it tries to head into the weeds. At first you think it's a bass, but then the sideways fighting style of the fish lets you know that it is a bluegill, and a big one at that, perhaps the biggest you have ever caught. . . .

You're vacationing in Yellowstone National Park and you want to fish for trout. You've planned a number of hikes into both the better-known and lesser-known streams. In the morning, you take a mile-long hike with your backpack down to the Yellowstone River, but it is high and roily here and you know that if you cast into the powerful current your fly will just be swept away. However, you notice a small, swirling eddy about two feet across right by the shore, caused by a large rock at the edge of the river and, as you stare into the water, you think you see flashes of white. You tie on a dark spruce streamer and flip it into the swirling eddy (no cast necessary). You feel a sudden jolt and hook into a hard fighting 14-inch cutthroat. . . .

You slowly meander along the accessible bank of a lake in a state park near your home. There is wildlife to be seen here: osprey and bald eagles fishing over the lake, bullfrogs croaking, water snakes, turtles, and so many birds. And there are fish, and you never know what will go for your fly. If you are lucky, you might catch a largemouth bass, black crappie, pickerel, and sunfish, all on the same fly. And every cast brings adventure and mystery. . . .

Although these situations vary in a number of ways (close to home vs. vacationing, focus on general outdoor activities vs. a singular focus on fishing, or coldwater vs. warmwater fishing), they all involve fly fishing using only

Traveling light: a backpack and a fly rod.

equipment that fits into a medium-sized daypack. Backpack fly fishing offers a minimalist, simplified, back-to-basics approach to the sport that is flexible and adaptable to multiple situations. For me, this approach evolved in part from the realities of traveling on vacations with my family with limited car space. However, it also emerged from the desire to simplify fly fishing and to get back to what I first loved about it, unencumbered by all of the equipment that I had come to feel was always necessary.

Why Backpack Fly Fishing?

Let's be clear before we go any further: I am not advocating the approach described here as the *only* approach to fishing. Certainly, there are times when I want to fly fish with my full vest and chest waders, or spin fish for bass with rubber worms. But backpack fly fishing is a unique and enjoyable alternative, and I have found that I like having this option to turn to. In fact, I find myself turning to backpack fly fishing more and more.

There are a number of compelling reasons for using this approach:

1. ***Simplicity and Getting Back to Basics:*** When I started fly fishing in my late twenties, I used the fiberglass 7-weight fly rod that Kathy had given me as a surprise gift and a handful of store-bought flies in a clear plastic box. Half a lifetime later, I own eight fly rods (five of which I built), a vest loaded with different fly boxes and other equipment, and three pairs of waders, not

to mention a full arsenal of fly-tying equipment. I have enjoyed all of this equipment over the years, but often I want to get back to the *feeling* of that first fly rod and fly box. Backpack fly fishing is a perfect way to get back to that sense of simplicity, when you choose to do so. (Incidentally, I caught a surprising variety of fish, including several "personal best" records, on that first fly rod and a handful of flies). For me, backpack fly fishing helps me get back to the allure of a fly rod and reel and the wonder of seeing or feeling fish take a beautifully tied fly.

2. ***Versatility of Fly Fishing:*** Some people associate fly fishing primarily with coldwater species such as trout or salmon. Fly fishing, however, is an *extremely versatile* approach to catching fish. I am not a particularly gifted or skilled fisherman (as my friend Tom will attest), but, using a fly rod, I have caught brook, brown, rainbow, and cutthroat trout, smallmouth and largemouth bass, bluegills and other sunfish, crappies (calico bass), yellow perch, Atlantic salmon, landlocked salmon, striped bass, shad, and bluefish. Most of these were caught on medium-weight fly rods (sizes 5 to 7), and many of these were caught while I was only carrying a single box of flies in my backpack.

3. ***Not Species Specific:*** Sometimes, I want to fish for a specific type of fish in a certain river or lake. At other times, however, I just want to fish and see what I dis-

cover. Backpack fly fishing is perfect for those situations. Let me give you an example. Recently, I fished a popular stream that is stocked with trout during the spring and fall. Tom had told me that there were possible holdover trout in the stream, but also smallmouth bass and bluegills. I fished the stream in the late July heat as Kathy watched for birds and, although no trout were in evidence, I caught a smallmouth bass and some nice bluegills. I may go back to that stream to fish specifically for trout once they stock it again, but on that occasion I was more than satisfied to prospect a bit, get to know the stream, and catch wild fish.

4. *Different Types of Water:* Rivers, streams, small ponds, and large lakes all present different challenges and offer different rewards. I enjoy adapting my casting, fly selection, and fly retrieval strategies to different situations. Fishing for warmwater fish like bass or bluegills hiding underneath stands of lily pads along the shoreline of a lake calls for a different approach than you would take when fishing for trout along a small forest stream. Also, because of the nature of backpack fly fishing, you sometimes need to work around the limitations of this approach. For example, although it is certainly easier to fish a lake from a boat or canoe, I enjoy trying to figure out when and how to catch fish from shore without much, if any, wading. Casting into still water requires different line mending and retrieval techniques than fishing into faster moving, complex

Beaver lodge on a warmwater pond.

currents in a small or medium-sized stream. More-
over, it is enjoyable and satisfying to spend time on
different types of water (sometimes during the same
day), with their varied birdlife, trees, shrubs, and insects. For example, think of the beauty of watching a
mayfly or caddis fly rise from a stream, and then consider the sight of large dragonflies attacking smaller
insects at dusk on a misty lake.

5. ***Combining Fishing with Other Activities:*** Recently,
Kathy and I got up early to go to one of our favorite
lakes. I brought my backpack and fly rod and she her
binoculars. I caught a couple of small bass, but the fishing was slow. The bird-watching, on the other hand,

was not, and when I took a break, Kathy showed me the photos she had taken of a pair of orioles and some cedar waxwings. She also thought that she had spotted a pair of yellow-bellied sapsuckers. I put down my fly rod and started to join her in bird-watching and, although the orioles had left, I saw the waxwings and then spotted an osprey searching for fish over the lake. The next time we go to that lake, I will keep my binoculars handy.

Many activities are often concurrent when I am carrying my backpack and fly rod:

- hiking
- picnicking
- identifying wildflowers
- identifying trees or shrubs
- bird-watching
- camping
- and any number of other activities

I consider it to be fishing within the context of another activity, and I find that these other activities enhance my enjoyment of fishing.

6. ***Fishing with People Who Don't Fish:*** Related to the advantage that I just described is the enjoyment of fishing while spending time with people who don't. On the occasion described above, I fished, Kathy watched for birds, and we shared the experience of enjoying an early morning at the lake. Many entries in

my fishing journal over the years contain comments such as "while hiking with Kathy and the boys . . .", "while camping together . . .", "Kathy found and photographed wildflowers . . .", "Brendan and Zach looked for fossils . . .", and so forth. On each of these occasions, I had the opportunity to fish while the people I was with engaged in other outdoor activities.

7. ***The Creativity of Fly Tying:*** This last advantage, in fairness, is not unique to *backpack* fly fishing, as it is an advantage to fly fishing in general. In any case, I have always been drawn to fly fishing in large part because I love tying flies. On so many days when you can't or don't fish, you can still be involved with the sport. It is particularly enjoyable to make adaptations to existing fly patterns or create your own based on your observations, or even just on a whim. My favorite dry fly is a Hairwing Henryville Special, which is my adaptation of the traditional Henryville Special caddis fly imitation. I simply replaced the duck quill wing with higher-visibility, more durable, and easier-to-tie white synthetic hair fibers. When my sons were young and tried tying flies for a while, they each invented their own streamer pattern and I still tie and use them both. They are the Blue Sunrise (Zach's fly) and the Green Glitterer (Brendan's fly). Both have caught trout and work with other fish also, and they are unique results of my sons' creativity. (See chapter 6 for tying instructions for these flies.)

Imitating this damsel fly would be a fly-tying challenge.

Some Assumptions Underlying This Book

I am approaching this topic with three assumptions in mind:

First, I am assuming that you as a reader already have some familiarity with the sport of fly fishing. This book is not an introduction to fly fishing, and there are many books available to the beginner to get you started. This book extends that information by describing how you can use your foundational skills in a unique and enjoyable way.

Second, I am assuming that people have different reasons for wanting to learn about and use the strategies described here. Some may be flyfishers primarily who, like myself, want to simplify the process. Others may be seri-

Wild trout along a forest stream.

ous hikers who encounter lakes and rivers in their long travels and would like to explore what lies beneath the waters. Still others may be nature lovers who want to add fly fishing to their fun outdoor pursuits. And, finally, others may be fishers who simply want to do more fly fishing but without an extensive commitment of money.

Third, I am assuming that readers may live in different locations in the United States and elsewhere. Different climates, conditions, terrains, and weather patterns mean different fish and strategies to pursue them. As a result, the ideas and strategies contained here will need to be tailored to where you live. Fortunately, backpack fly fishing is a highly adaptable approach that works in a vast range of situations and is not bound by geography.

Summary

All of the reasons described above have led me to enjoy backpack fly fishing more and more, often above other approaches. This approach offers an alternative way to enjoy fishing that can be freer than other approaches but just as effective, sometimes more so. In fact, in the near future I have scheduled an exclusive opportunity to fish two beats of a local private trout stream, using my full fishing vest and waders, but I have also planned a trip back to the lake with Kathy to fish for crappies, bluegills, and bass. Although the trout stream could be interesting, I find myself looking forward more to the trip back to the lake.

Chapter Two

ASCAL in Action:
The Backpack Fly-Fishing Process

This book does not introduce a revolutionary or entirely new way of fly fishing. If I had developed such an innovation that changed the face of the sport, you would have already heard about it but, alas, I have not. What I have done is taken known and familiar tactics of fly fishing and simplified them into an easy-to-remember and easy-to-use set of steps. I call this the ASCAL method:

Approach
Select
Cast
Animate
Land

These steps, which are described in this chapter, apply to *any situation* that we might encounter. The steps are not magic, but how we implement each step is highly dependent on the situation. How we complete the five steps of the ASCAL method on a small forest trout stream will be different from how we would implement them on a large warmwater lake. Knowing the steps helps us to analyze situations that we encounter and creates the best opportunities for catching fish. We will look at the steps in action in different places and situations in chapter 5, but for now, let's look at each part of the ASCAL method.

The Five Steps of the ASCAL Method

STEP 1: APPROACH

The first thing that we need to do in any potential fishing situation is to carefully approach the water. For many

Approaching a promising area from below.

flyfishers, this is where the first mistakes can occur as they approach a stream or pond too loudly and quickly and scare away potential fish before they have even had a chance to cast for them. So, the first rule of thumb in approaching water is to *look first and then approach slowly.*

If I am hiking and come upon a stream, river, or pond, I stop and look as soon as I see the water. I hold still and let my eyes take in everything with as little sound and movement as possible. If it is a brook, stream, or river, I determine the direction in which the water is flowing and look for any possible lies for fish to hide (for example, downstream of rocks or boulders, under undercut banks, etc.), and I look for "seams" in the stream where slow water and fast water meet, for fish will often congregate there. I try to keep my footfalls as light as possible as I advance to take a better look, because fish can feel the vibrations caused by heavier steps.

If I approach a pond or lake, I look for areas that are more accessible from the banks with fewer overhanging trees or shrubs. I also look for structure in the water, such as stands of lily pads, sandbars, or half-submerged logs. If possible, I look into the water to see where shallow water drops off into deeper water. It may also be necessary to stoop down and keep a low profile so that I don't spook fish that are conditioned to view shadows from above as possible predatory threats.

Although I may need to get fairly close to the water to assess the conditions, once I have done so I try to back

Where would fish be located?

away so that my completion of the next step does not scare away possible fish.

STEP 2: SELECT

Select a fly, that is, based on what we have observed in Step 1. Now, the backpack fly-fishing method is based on the assumption that we are carrying a smaller collection of flies that have a chance of being useful in a fairly wide range of situations. Although we will address the selection of flies that are appropriate to your area in greater detail in chapters 4 and 6, for now suffice it to say that this means that we will have one well-stocked fly box with our *best selection of tried-and-true flies in which we have the greatest confidence.* This selection of one's personal favorites is

Some essential flies.

just that, personal. It is therefore shaped by our personal experiences and by the types of waters to which we gravitate and the fish that live in them. For me, these are the flies that immediately come to mind when I think of the question: "If I were stuck in an isolated area that had good fishing, what flies would I *definitely* want with me?"

To some degree, flies become personal favorites because we fish with them more often, which, of course, increases the likelihood that they have a chance of working, thereby reinforcing our high opinion of them. Maybe we just fish with more confidence with them, which means that we will persist longer in trying to catch fish. Whatever the reasons that we favor them, these flies are our personal selection that we feel are indispensible. Keep in mind, however, that we are typically restricted by room to carrying no more than three or four of each of these personal favorites. Also, assuming that you want to be ready to fish a fairly wide range of situations, then you need to keep your selection of flies that are for specific situations (for example, trout on small streams or largemouth bass in a lake or pond) to a restricted number of flies.

STEP 3: CAST

Next, we need to cast the fly to where the fish may be waiting. Advanced fly-fishing books cover numerous specialty casts that allow a flyfisher to respond to any number of situations. I know almost none of these and never will.

I do know, however, three basic casts that are reliable and useful. These are a standard overhand cast, a side-

A basic overhand cast.

arm cast, and a roll cast. I use the first two for about 99 percent of my casting, in part because I am a terrible roll caster. But, in general, these casts have served me well in just about any situation that I have encountered. (It is not my intent here to digress into a casting lesson, and I am undoubtedly not the best person to give it anyway, so refer to a beginning fly-fishing book for instructions on these and other casts.)

I have also found that long-distance power casts are rarely necessary. Good thing, because I can't do those either! Typically, most of my casts are fairly short, say twenty to thirty feet, perhaps a bit longer. There have certainly been times when I have *wished* that I could cast out to the middle of a lake to rising fish but, then again, there will be other times when I can go canoeing and catch fish in the middle, so I don't spend time worrying about fish I can't reach. Instead, I would rather focus on those that may be closer than we think.

One additional comment about casting: try to minimize situations in which poor handling of the line scares fish away. I have made enough bad casts, sloppy retrieves, and so forth to at least be aware of these ahead of time so that I can try to avoid them whenever possible.

STEP 4: ANIMATE

To animate a fly means to make it look like a living creature. For a caddis or mayfly imitation in a trout stream, this may mean doing nothing but letting the fly drift without drag, because that is what the natural insects may be doing. If you

An enticing bass bug.

are animating a nymph swimming from the streambed to the surface, then a nymph imitation that is allowed to sink and then be retrieved to the surface may look more natural. A bass bug that is twitched on the surface of a still pond and then is allowed to sit motionless before twitching again may look alive and vulnerable to a hungry bass or pickerel. A streamer fly that is designed to look like a minnow or small fish may trigger a strike if it is retrieved in short, erratic pulls that look like the movement of an injured fish.

Animating a fly is one of the most enjoyable aspects of fly fishing. For me, it ensures that I am an active participant in the process, not simply someone who is waiting for a fish to come along and take the bait. (This is one of the reasons why bait fishing has never thrilled me much, however effective it might be in different situations). It is the casting and fly animation elements of fly fishing that make it an active and highly participatory approach to fishing. It is fun and challenging to make a bass bug look alive, or to make a streamer really look like an injured minnow. At times, I get so into animating a fly that I temporarily forget why I am doing it! I find myself studying what streamers or wet flies look like as they come through the water, and I try different speeds of retrieval to make them look more alive. It really can be a fun and engrossing way of engaging the imaginative mind as well as (hopefully) the fish!

STEP 5: LAND

Although the broader reason for fishing is to have fun and enjoy time outdoors, a more focused goal is to catch fish (and then release them). In this sense, to "land" a fish means to hook it, fight it, subdue it, bring it to hand, and then release it back into its home waters where it can live to fight again.

The first challenge is to hook the fish. For most situations, the key is to react as soon as you detect a strike. Some fish tend to hook themselves, such as a trout, bass, or pickerel striking a streamer or wet fly stripped in fast, but others do not, and you need to react quickly. For example, a trout or bluegill hitting a dry fly can and will spit it out quickly, as soon as it recognizes that your fly is not a natural insect. (Bluegills are incredibly fast at this and can inhale and then exhale a fly faster than you can say "pop"! That's one of the many reasons I love fishing for them.) A bass hitting a bass bug on top or a slow-moving underwater streamer will, likewise, exhale it as soon as it detects

Releasing a brown trout.

something unnatural. So, in general, the key is to strike as soon as you detect a possible hit. For a trout or bluegill, this means raising the rod tip to hook the fish. For a bass, this entails striking by pulling hard on the line with your retrieval hand while raising the rod horizontally and back to set the hook, as suggested by Dave Whitlock. Keep in mind that this is often where fish are lost, and nothing is more frustrating than a nice fish that was briefly on but then got off.

How we land a fish depends a lot on the type of fish that we catch and how big it is. Largemouth bass are my favorite to land because, once I have a hold of their lower jaw, I can remove the hook and release them quickly and efficiently. Not so with pickerel or other toothed fish, or

Landing a largemouth bass.

with larger trout. In these situations, wetting your landing hand and *gently* holding the fish's body while you remove the hook with a pair of pliers works best. If I am landing a large bluegill, I make sure to hold it with my palm on its belly, because its dorsal fins are sharp and can really hurt. This is also true of yellow perch. Barbless hooks remove more easily with less damage to fish, so these are a must. Although a net would be helpful in some situations, in the backpacking fly-fishing approach, it is extra equipment that I don't carry.

Fish should be released as soon as possible. If you want to measure the fish and possibly photograph it, try to do so quickly with minimal handling of the fish. (I measure almost all fish I catch and photograph selected ones, and I then keep track of that information in my fishing journal.) Then put the fish back into the water until it swims away under its own power.

Errors and the ASCAL Method

It is very easy to make mistakes in fly fishing that cost us the opportunity to catch memorable fish. In fact, most of us remember fish that got away, and those are the times that we relive in our minds, imagining what we would have done differently. Although we cannot prevent all errors from occurring, it is helpful to look out for common mistakes in the completion of each of the five steps of the ASCAL method.

During the *approach* step, the most common mistakes are to spook fish by walking too closely to the water, stepping too heavily and causing vibrations that fish feel, or leaning out over the water so that fish see your shadow from above. All of these will spook fish and end a good fishing opportunity before you have even started. Instead, always approach slowly and carefully and take note of what you see happening on the water.

During the *select* step, one error is to pick a fly that has little chance for success. If you see flies hatching on a stream or lake, and you note that fish seem to be going after them, then it makes sense to select flies that most closely resemble the insects that you see. Sometimes, fish can be extremely selective about what they will eat and only flies that resemble natural foods will be effective. Other times, it does not seem to matter as much, and almost any fly might work. However, you should not use flies that are too big for particular fish. For example, bluegills are more likely to go after small cork or deer hair poppers than large-sized bass bugs designed for large-mouth bass.

Numerous errors can occur during *casting*, and fly-fishers spend years trying to improve their casting abilities. The most common errors are to bring the rod too far back on the back cast, thereby causing a more open loop in the fly line and losing power on the forward cast. It takes timing and practice to ensure that the fly rod is "loading," or flexed due to the pull of the fly line on the back cast (so that the person using the rod is not overworking during the casting process). A second major error is to make splashy, loud casts that smack the water and scare fish away. Try to cast with minimal splashing so that the fly lands near a fish but not right over its head.

During the *animation* step, the key is to know when and when not to actively move a fly. If mayflies and other insects are drifting on the surface of a trout stream, then pulling a dry fly across the water or allowing it to drag in the current will look unnatural to a trout and they will likely ignore the fly. Likewise, a deer hair bass bug that is designed to look like a frog should move erratically to look realistic. The fly should not only look like a natural food, but it should *act* like one.

Finally, during the *land* step, the most important things to keep in mind are to control the fish, remove the hook, and release the fish as quickly as possible. Like everything else, this takes practice. I have learned a lot over the years about how to land different kinds of fish as quickly and efficiently as possible. As mentioned above, some fish have sharp dorsal fin spines, and others have sharp teeth, and all of these can inflict injuries if you are not careful. Also, it takes practice to control fish and release them without squeezing them too hard, dropping them, or keeping them out of the water too long.

Summary

The ASCAL method (Approach, Select, Cast, Animate, Land) is not a new way to fly fish. Rather, it is a framework or template to be used to guide us in how to deal with the varied situations that we encounter while backpack fly fishing. We will discuss several different examples of the

ASCAL method in action in chapter 5, but for now, let's turn our attention to the variety of fish that you might encounter and enjoy pursuing and catching while using this approach.

Chapter Three

What's the Catch
The Fish and Where and How They Live

One of the allures of backpack fly fishing is that it is based on a philosophy of non-specialization and a realization that all fish offer their own beauty and challenges. In that respect, backpack fly fishing is a generalist's sport that requires that we know about a range of fish and how to catch them. These different fish live in different environments that, like the fish themselves, have their own unique beauties.

When I started fly fishing, I went through fairly predictable stages. First, I wanted to catch *anything* on a fly rod, which translated to bluegills and other panfish that (under certain conditions) seemed to be easier to catch. I then "progressed" to trout and began to think of them as the only worthy fish. Later, I became enthralled with the concept of catching largemouth bass on a fly rod. Along the way, I also dabbled in Atlantic salmon fishing on the rare occasions that I found myself on a salmon river in Nova Scotia, and I even had the opportunity to fly fish on coastal waters for small stripers and bluefish on the Rhode

Island shore. But, ultimately, I realized that *all* fish were beautiful, interesting, and challenging, in their own ways. I have often thought that a wild brook trout is the most beautiful fish, but then when I catch a common sunfish (pumpkin seed) with its vibrant and iridescent colors, I change my mind, at least for that moment.

Freshwater Fish

BLUEGILLS AND SUNFISH

Bluegills and other sunfish are my first love and I still find them to be challenging adversaries. There are many species of sunfish, but I typically encounter bluegills and their colorful cousins, common sunfish or pumpkin seeds. One

A bluegill: the perfect fly rod quarry.

of the most distinguishing characteristics of sunfish is their strong fight with a sideways swimming action that makes the most of their wide body shape. They are terrific fun on a light or medium fly rod, and I am never disappointed to catch a good-sized bluegill. (By the way, what is a "good-sized" bluegill? As in most things, it depends on where you live. In their excellent book *Bluegill Fly Fishing and Flies*, Terry and Roxanne Wilson define a "larger" bluegill as anything of 8 inches or longer. My own personal best bluegill is 9.5 inches, but I still hope for a double-digit bluegill someday).

I have caught bluegills in two ways: with dead-drifted dry flies or with wet flies stripped in as quickly as possible. Fishing for bluegills with dry flies is one of the most fun

A colorful common sunfish, or pumpkinseed.

ways to fly fish. This is particularly so in the spring when they are on their nests in the shallow waters of lakes or ponds. They are FAST, so your reaction time in striking has to be accurate. Fishing dry flies for bluegills was my first fly-fishing experience, and it is still one of the most enjoyable and humbling approaches to fly fishing. You are never too old for it!

Wet fly fishing is also productive, particularly with standard wet flies, such as the Dark Cahill, the Professor, the Coachman, or other traditional wet flies. A particularly successful wet fly is the Wilsons' Bully's Bluegill Spider, described in their book (mentioned above). I once had an outing during which I caught a 13.5-inch largemouth bass, a 7.5-inch bluegill, and a 7.5-inch crappie, all on the same bluegill spider. I am not sure why the Wilsons' Bully's Bluegill Spider works, but it definitely does. I have had to tie them myself because I could not find any in the local stores around me. The fun part of using wet flies is to retrieve them by stripping them in fairly quickly with short, erratic pulls on the fly line. Many times the variations in retrieval speeds seem to trigger strikes. But bluegills and other sunfish can also be maddeningly picky and wary when fished for with wet flies, as they can with dry flies.

CRAPPIES (CALICO BASS)

Crappies are related to bluegills and other sunfish but are typically larger. There are two varieties: the black and white crappie. In some areas, they are often referred to as "calico bass," which is a descriptive term that captures

Calico bass or crappie.

their color well. They are often schooling fish, so if you catch one, you might well have a chance at another. I have caught them in ponds and lakes that hold other warmwater fish such as bass, bluegills, and pickerel. I have mostly caught them on fast-moving streamers, wet flies, and nymphs stripped in quickly. They are always a surprise when you are fishing for sunfish, because they are larger and heavier. They are also downright beautiful, with their silver-white iridescence and black markings. Calico bass have delicate mouths, so it is easy for a hook to pull loose; therefore, they need to be landed carefully. My personal best calico bass, caught on an early successful fly-fishing trip to White City Lake in Trenton, New Jersey, with Tom so many years ago, was 13.5 inches—a great fish!

PERCH

I have caught yellow perch, but mostly when trying for bluegills or bass. These fish are beautiful and colorful, with their orange fins and yellow bodies. My largest to

Yellow perch.

date on a fly rod was 10 inches, caught on a streamer fly.
When I have caught them, it is because they were chasing
a quickly stripped wet or streamer fly that was intended to
imitate a minnow.

LARGEMOUTH AND SMALLMOUTH BASS

These two great game fish live in somewhat different environments. Largemouth bass tend to inhabit warmwater
ponds and lakes that offer lots of cover, such as lily pads,
weeds, and sunken logs. Smallmouth bass inhabit cooler
water and can often be found in streams, rivers, or cooler
lakes. Both are tremendous fun to catch on a fly rod.

My most memorable catch of a smallmouth bass occurred in central Pennsylvania, where I was camping with
my family a number of years ago. A noted trout stream
flowed from the north into the lake at the campground,
and then the stream continued out of the lake below the
dammed lower end. I tried fishing this lower section with
a pack fly rod and a Black Ghost Marabou streamer. I

Smallmouth bass.

walked down to the river's edge in my shorts to scout out the river. There was a seam of fast water on the far side and slower water near my side. The road into the campground crossed a bridge across the creek. As I started to fish, I noticed an older gentleman up on the bridge to my left who had stopped to watch me fish. I cast to the far bank into the seam between the faster and slower water and then stripped the fly in rather quickly. I was rewarded with three hard fighting and leaping smallmouths, all about 10 inches long—a great fight on a light fly rod! The man on the bridge shouted down to me, "Looks like someone's having a lot of fun!"

A NOTE ON "PERSONAL BESTS"

You will note that some of mine are not all that big or impressive, but guess what? It doesn't matter because they were (a) MY personal bests and (b) all terrific fun! They also keep me striving for new personal bests to come!

Largemouth bass.

Largemouth bass are great fun to catch on bass bugs. (For more on this topic, read Dave Whitlock's book, *LL Bean Fly Fishing for Bass Handbook,* and William G. Tapply's book, *Bass Bug Fishing.* Both are indispensible references on strategies and techniques for largemouth bass.) There is something incredibly fun about casting out a bass bug or popper, animating it a little, and then *waiting . . .* Sometimes nothing happens, but at other times when things are going your way, the bug explodes in a smashing hit of a bass on top and the battle is engaged. As Tapply states, in bass fishing this is "the moment"!

Although largemouth bass can be caught on subsurface flies, most people tend to enjoy fishing for them on top with hard- or soft-bodied bass bugs. This is also fun because in a warmwater pond or lake, particularly those

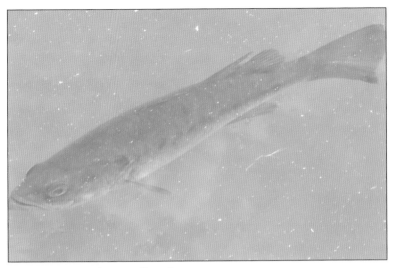

A largemouth bass in a small pond.

with stands of lily pads and other aquatic vegetation that provide cover for fish, you have the potential to catch bass, good sized bluegills, calico bass, or pickerel. I enjoy fishing warmwater ponds because of this unpredictability, which adds excitement to the experience.

PICKEREL

Chain pickerel are among the smallest of the pike family. Their larger cousins include northern pike and muskellunge. I have seen photographs of anglers who have caught these on large bass flies and heavier fly rods, but I have not had that pleasure. I have, however, enjoyed catching pickerel on streamers and other underwater flies. I remember my friend Tom telling me that pickerel will often follow a lure or fly right up to a boat or shore before striking, and I have now experienced that as well. It can be quite a sur-

Pickerel.

prise to have a fish strike the fly right before you are ready to cast again. Although some bass fishers look down on pickerel, I find them to be fascinating creatures with their snake-like bodies and duckbill-shaped mouths full of sharp teeth. My largest so far on a fly rod is 16.75 inches, but I would love to catch one of 18 inches or better. They have a primeval and fearsome look to them, and they can put up a strong fight. When landing and releasing pickerel, or any member of the pike family, it is important to take care to avoid their sharp teeth.

TROUT

Where I live in Pennsylvania, the major trout species are brook, brown, and rainbow trout. In the West, I have also caught cutthroat trout. All are beautiful and challenging, each in their own ways.

Although not large, wild (and in the East, native) brook trout are among the most beautiful fish of the fly-fishing world. A 7- or 8-inch wild brook trout is a thing of beauty and is typically found in some of the most beautiful

A wild Nova Scotia brook trout.

places, such as small streams with lots of oxygenating plunge pools and mini-waterfalls or in wild northern lakes, such as those in the Maritime provinces of Canada. Some of my favorite memories are walking through forests in Cape Breton Highlands National Park in Nova Scotia, fishing for wild brook trout (or "speckled trout," as they are known there) with traditional wet flies. In fact, it was on these streams that the initial idea for this book was born. (More on fishing in Cape Breton in chapter 5). No place and no other fish are more beautiful.

Many flyfishers consider brown trout to be the most selective and challenging of the trouts, and it is terrific fun to catch, particularly on a dry fly. I have had most success with small caddis fly imitations, because these flies are the most abundant ones that hatch on the small streams that I fish. As mentioned previously, my personal favorite fly is a variation of the Henryville Special, a fly first developed for the local Pocono Mountains area. My first Pennsylvania trout was an 11-inch brown caught on a small stream on a #18 Hairwing Henryville. I have also caught brown trout on nymphs, streamers, and wet flies.

Rainbow trout favor water a bit colder than browns, and I have mostly caught them in rivers and lakes, which have been stocked. One September day a few years ago, Kathy and I hiked into a local nature preserve along a beautiful Pocono stream called Tobyhanna Creek. As always, we brought our binoculars for bird-watching and I brought my backpack with my six-piece Cortland fly rod.

Brown trout.

Rainbow trout.

We hiked in to where large boulders offered a place to stop and admire the beauty of the river falls. I had taken a few idle casts here in the past and decided to do so again but with very few expectations other than to enjoy the day. I tied on a Beadhead Wooly Bugger because I like streamers, particularly in the fall. On my first cast and retrieve, I felt something bump the fly. It could have been a rock, but perhaps a fish. This looked like classic small-mouth bass water, and I hoped for a hard-fighting small-mouth bass. On my second cast, I hooked a nice fish that fought hard, jumping once. Although I had hoped for a hard-fighting smallmouth, I was happy to catch a 13-inch rainbow trout, a real beauty. Once again, I had not really intended to go fishing that day, only hiking to take a few photos and look for birds. The beautiful trout was a bonus on a relaxing fall hike on a stream.

In the western United States, cutthroat trout offer tremendous fun. As an Easterner, even the name cutthroat trout epitomized the rugged West to me when I first fished in Montana. Cutthroat trout are typically larger than East Coast brook trout, and their distinctive slashed-throat markings and overall coloration are distinctive and quite beautiful. My most memorable catch of cutthroats occurred during a hatch of pale morning duns on Yellowstone Lake, during which the trout fed selectively on emerging flies, while diving white pelicans fed on the trout.

WHITEFISH

Whitefish are related to trout and tend to inhabit the same types of environments. The first and only whitefish that I caught was from a drift boat on the Yellowstone River in Montana. The fishing was terrible that day and, as I recall, mine was the only catch of the day for two of us. I remember being disappointed that it was not my first Montana trout, but I should have better appreciated its beauty and its fight. Whitefish are shaped similarly to a trout but have overall whitish color. In my home state of Pennsylvania, the lake whitefish is an important commercial fish native to Lake Erie (*Pennsylvania Fishes*, 2000).

Saltwater Coastal Fish

Although I have focused on freshwater fish in describing the backpack fly-fishing approach in this book, the process applies equally well to saltwater fish found along the coasts. Also, saltwater fish typically put up a stronger fight than do freshwater fish, so a small striped bass or bluefish on a medium- or even heavy-weight fly rod can be terrific fun. It is only necessary to carry a handful of streamer patterns, such as Clouser Deep Minnows or Epoxy Eels. Often, you can detect where they might be by observing gulls, terns, and other birds congregating in a certain area, or by seeing schools of minnows jumping out of the water in a vain attempt to escape the pursuing fish. These coastal fish are subject to seasonal variations that determine when they are in particular areas of the coast. For example, in the Northeast and Mid-Atlantic regions, the striped bass and bluefish typically start to appear during the spring and then leave for their southern migration in the fall. Even within the United States, there are many regional variations of fish that are found near the coasts, and it is beyond the scope of this book to go into all of these possibilities. However, on the Northeast and Mid-Atlantic coasts, where I have had some experiences with coastal backpack fly fishing, the two particular species described below stand out.

STRIPED BASS

Striped bass are beautiful and hard-fighting saltwater fish. They are generally white with black horizontal lines along their flanks. Although serious striper fishers go for the large fish in the 15 to 20 pound range, smaller stripers or "schoolies" along the coast can be caught in harbors, inlets, and other areas close to shore and within easy wet wading and casting range. As with all saltwater fish along the shore areas, the best times for an opportunity to catch these fish are on a high tide or one that is incoming and almost high. The fish follow the smaller fish as the incoming tide brings them closer to shore. Although small by the standards of serious saltwater fishers, the 21-inch striper that I caught within a foot or two of water right in front of my parents' home in Rhode Island is a fish that I will not forget.

BLUEFISH

Bluefish are vicious fish that attack and slash with their sharp teeth. In larger sizes, up to approximately 20 pounds, bluefish are highly sought out quarry of serious saltwater anglers. In smaller sizes, from about 6 to 8 inches, they are hard-fighting, bluegill-sized, piranha-like fish that will eagerly attack a streamer fly that is retrieved with a panic strip. In Rhode Island, these fish are referred to as skip-jacks, while in New Jersey they are called snapper blues. Regardless of the name used, they are incredible fun and

Bluefish.

surprisingly hard fighting for their size. Because of their sharp teeth, they fray and cut leaders easily, so use a heavier leader and bring extras. They also dismantle flies easily, so make sure to bring enough. One strategy that I tried with success while fishing with my sons in the harbor by my parents' home was to troll (while rowing our dinghy) with a Clouser Deep Minnow and a smaller Mickey Finn dropper fly behind it. The small bluefish consistently went for the smaller fly, and we caught several that day, including one that wriggled off the hook and fell into the pant leg opening of my shorts, which, of course, was the highlight of the day for my young sons.

Anadromous Fish

Although the chances are far less that you will have an opportunity to fish for these migratory fish, it is worth touching on them here. Anadromous fish are those that spawn in fresh water and then migrate to the oceans to live. They then return to their natal rivers to spawn once they reach adulthood. In Canada's Atlantic Provinces (Nova Scotia, New Brunswick, Prince Edward Island, and Newfoundland and Labrador) and in Quebec, Atlantic salmon are the principle anadromous fish. Because of their declining numbers, fishing is restricted to fly fishing only, and most places require the fisher to hire a local guide. Opportunities for backpack fly fishing are quite restricted, although it is possible to do so in Nova Scotia's Cape Breton Highlands National Park, where (as of this writing) guides are not required. (More on this in chapter 5.) Atlantic salmon are the "kings" of fly fishing, due to their potentially large size and their incredible leaping ability, and the history of fly fishing is replete with colorful attractor flies (streamers) from the British Isles, Canada, and the United States. Due to declines in salmon runs, fishing for Atlantic salmon is no longer allowed in the United States, and extensive restoration projects are underway in Maine.

On the Pacific coast, the coho, chinook, and other Pacific salmon also live in salt water but then enter fresh water to spawn. Unlike Atlantic salmon, which may live to return to the ocean to spawn again, Pacific salmon die after spawning. Some Pacific salmon, specifically the coho, chinook, and pink salmon, have been introduced successfully into the Great Lakes.

A relative of the Atlantic salmon is the landlocked salmon. These are anatomically identical to Atlantic salmon, but they live in large freshwater lakes and then return to their natal rivers to spawn (Thompson, 1980). For example, landlocked salmon runs occur in Vermont and New York state as landlocked salmon leave Lake Champlain in the spring and fall to enter rivers on both sides of the lake to spawn.

Trout that live near salt water can also adopt anadromous behavior. Sea run brook, brown, and rainbow trout can grow to larger than typical sizes in salt water. Anadromous brook and brown trout are referred to as "salters" or "sea trout" (Thompson, 1980), and anadromous rainbow trout are called steelhead. Trout that enter salt or brackish water to live typically turn a duller shade of color, so that sea run trout will be more of a steel greyish color than those found in freshwater.

The East Coast of the United States also is home to American shad, which are the major anadromous fish of the Northeast. For example, spring shad runs are long awaited events in places such as the Delaware River, the last major undammed river on the East Coast, and shad festivals take place in numerous river towns. Shad fisherman typically spin fish with weighted shad "darts," but some fly fish for these hard-fighting fish.

Although opportunities for backpack fly fishing for anadromous fish are far less likely than they are for trout, bass, or other warmwater fish, if you live near the coast, on major lakes, or near larger rivers, it is possible that you might have a chance to go for one of these fascinating and challenging fish.

Which Fish Is the Best Fish?

Too many times, flyfishers have ranked fish according to their desirability. Table 3.1 shows my interpretation of this traditional way of thinking. Generally, according to this ranking system, coldwater fish, specifically trout and salmon, are considered to be superior to warmwater fish such as bass or pickerel. For example, Dave Whitlock referred to an "inherited narrow-mindedness" that prevented flyfishers from even considering fly fishing for bass. Also, within the category of the trout, brown trout are typically valued more highly than brook trout. Smallmouth bass are often thought of as superior to largemouth

TABLE 3.1
Traditional Fish Desirability Hierarchy

Trout & Salmon
(Brown trout, Atlantic salmon followed by
Landlocked salmon, Rainbow and Cutthroat trout, followed
by
Brook trout)

Saltwater Fish
(Striped bass, bonefish, followed by
Bluefish and other saltwater fish)

Bass
(Smallmouth, followed by
Largemouth bass)

Pikes and Pickerel
(Muskellunge, followed by
Northern Pike, followed by
Pickerel)

Sunfish

bass, because they tend to live in environments that are similar to those of trout. Interestingly, as saltwater fly fishing gained popularity over the past fifteen years or so, it has taken its place near the top of the hierarchy, just below trout, and clearly above bass. Simply peruse a current catalog of one of the major fly-fishing equipment companies and look at the photos that they provide to try to entice people to buy their products. You will find lots of photos of people fishing on streams for trout or catching trout (usually brown trout), and you will also find people catching saltwater fish, typically striped bass or bonefish. Rarely, if ever, will you find a photo of a person catching a bass, and you will never find a picture of someone catching a bluegill.

There is an alternative way of thinking about possible fish to catch. This alternative is based on the range of opportunities that present themselves to you in your travels and *not* on the relative "importance" or desirability of different types of fish. As shown in Table 3.2, this alternative simply recognizes that different fish live in different temperatures of water and different types of environments. (Note that freshwater fish and saltwater fish are considered separately.) This alternative way of thinking forces us to recognize that *all* fish are interesting and fun to catch under different circumstances. Certainly, some may be rarer or harder to catch, but that does not negate the value and interest of even "easy to catch" fish. A wild brook trout is a creature of intense beauty, but so is a bass, bluefish, or bluegill. No fish is better than another, simply

TABLE 3.2
Alternative Range of Opportunities Hierarchy

NOTE: This approach is based solely on which fish live in the environment that you encounter. This will be dictated largely by the type of water and the temperature of water on which you fish.

Fresh Water

Cold water	Cool water	Warm water
Trout	Smallmouth bass	Largemouth bass
Atlantic salmon	Walleye	Pickerel
Landlocked salmon	Pike	Sunfish, crappies
Whitefish	Sunfish	Yellow perch

Salt Water

Saltwater fish will be subject to migration patterns and, therefore, are locally variable. Typical options (depending on your location) include striped bass, redfish, and bluefish.

different. In learning to adopt this way of thinking, I have found it particularly interesting to get a hold of books that describe different fish, their characteristics, and their life cycles. Just as a bird-watcher studies different bird guides to help in identifying different birds, a flyfisher can and should do the same with fish. And, just as bird-watchers maintain a life list of birds that they have seen, flyfishers can and should maintain a life list of different fish that they have been fortunate enough to catch and identify.

Types of Water and Tactics

SMALL STREAMS

Smaller streams can be some of the most beautiful places to fish. My favorite small streams are in forests and woodland areas where houses are scarce. Often, the best small streams are well off the beaten path and may receive little fishing pressure. It is not unusual to come across a small stream that may not even have a name, or certainly not one that is well known. These streams are rarely stocked but may hold wild fish. They typically are not the ones you will find in guides to the best trout fishing in your state.

One of the things I like best about small streams is that they are microcosms of larger rivers. The ones I like

A promising looking pool on an isolated trout stream.

the best flow through rugged areas, with stair-step pools connected by riffles and mini-waterfalls. If the stream holds trout or any other fish, I like to cast a traditional wet fly, such as a Professor or a Coachman, into the base of the waterfall where the water is deepest and then quickly retrieve the fly in a panic strip. I have tried this on a number of occasions and caught many wild brook trout in that way. My personal best *smallest* brook trout was caught using this tactic in a beautiful small stream in northern Vermont: a beautiful 2.5-inch brook trout (the length of my little finger) that went for a #14 Professor almost a quarter of its own size. Gorgeous fish!

LARGER RIVERS

Larger rivers are challenging for different reasons and need to be approached differently. First, when I am backpack

The Chéticamp River, Nova Scotia.

fly fishing, I rarely am prepared to wade deep into a river, as I might do if I had chest waders. At most, I might wade to my ankles in bare feet or wading sandals, but more often than not I am casting from the shore. This means that good lies farther out on the river or on the other side are usually inaccessible. Instead, I look for pockets of water or back eddies that are near the shore and along the seam of the faster, main current. A streamer, wet fly, or nymph cast into these pockets can produce fish that might be waiting in the slower water, where they do not have to fight the current so much, while waiting for food to come along the main current. The 14-inch cutthroat trout that I caught on the Yellowstone River many years back, mentioned in chapter 1, was caught in this manner. Although the fish was literally right at my feet, I could not see it due to the water color and movement.

SMALLER PONDS

Due to their smaller size, small ponds tend to offer more fishable areas, assuming that some of the shoreline is accessible—and that, of course, is typically the first major challenge. Often, thick shrubs and trees line the shore of the pond and create barriers to getting to the pond itself and then casting. In these situations, it may be necessary to "bushwhack" your way through the shrubbery and then, once you get to the shoreline, use simple flip or roll casts. The good part about smaller ponds is that they typically receive very little fishing pressure, and you may find them along hiking trails. Again, a quickly stripped wet fly

A small pond at the edge of a meadow.

is a good way to search for fish, or a medium to small dry fly might be worth a try. I can recall catching a few fun bluegills and a very small bass using wet flies on a small pond in northern New Jersey while hiking and exploring with Kathy several years ago.

LARGE LAKES

As with large rivers, a backpack flyfisher needs to first identify areas of larger lakes that are actually going to be accessible and that might hold fish. I look for coves off the main lake and structures near the shore, such as lily pads, fallen logs, or brush piles. Most importantly is to accept that you are fishing the shoreline only and to be happy with that. Although fish will seek deeper and cooler water under a variety of circumstances, there are typically smaller fish near the shore. In warmwater lakes I have caught

Gouldsboro Lake, Pennsylvania.

bluegills, crappies, yellow perch, bass, and pickerel close to shore, and in coldwater lakes in the Maritime Provinces of Canada I have caught brook trout on small streamers and wet flies.

COASTAL AREAS

Coastal areas, inlets, coves, breakwaters, and beaches all offer potential areas for backpack fly fishing. You may want to take a stroll along a less crowded beach and try a few casts, particularly if you see birds hovering and congregating in a certain area. I have particularly enjoyed harbor areas where fish might be found on the incoming or high tides. Many times, these areas get very little fishing pressure, because most fishers are going for the big ones on boats out in the ocean or larger bays.

A saltwater estuary.

Summary

One of the great allures of backpack fly fishing is the pursuit of a wide variety of fish species in a range of different types of waters. If you know where you are headed, and you know that there is only one predominant species of fish there, then by all means enjoy the fishing. But, so many times, we do not know in advance where we will be fishing and what lives there, and that is the challenge and the fun in backpack fly fishing. Each of the fish described here, and many others that I have not described, have their own beauty, and each presents challenges that make fishing fun. Sometimes I will come across waters where I wish I had my canoe or my fully loaded vest and waders, but I could always do that another time. This time, I need to use my creativity to figure out what is in the stream, river, pond, lake, or cove, and then determine how to catch something using the minimal amount of equipment that I have in my backpack. If I catch anything, I admire its natural beauty and consider myself a success.

Chapter Four

Traveling Light
Equipment You Will and Will Not Need

Fishers like to collect stuff, and flyfishers like to collect LOTS of stuff. They wear vests with innumerable pockets to carry all of this stuff, and pretty soon they're afraid to fish without their heavily laden vests, just in case they might need a particular fly that has been waiting in a particular pocket of the vest for the past fifteen years.

Backpack fly fishing still involves stuff, but a lot less of it. As we have discussed, it is more of a minimalist approach that relies on our faith in a handful of flies that have done well in a variety of situations. This approach is based on the philosophy that, if it doesn't fit in a medium daypack, then we probably won't need it. However, even though backpack fly fishing relies on less stuff, it still needs to be the right stuff.

What You'll Need

In my experience, I have found the following to be important pieces of equipment for fun and successful backpack fly fishing:

- Backpack
- Flies
- Fly box
- Rod and reel
- Fly line and leaders
- Nippers/clippers
- Fleece patch
- Floatant
- Leatherman or pliers
- Sunglasses
- First aid kit
- Bandana
- License

Each of these is discussed further in the rest of this chapter.

BACKPACK

I prefer the simple, all-purpose daypack that many people use for school, college, or simply to lug stuff around. Mine is an Eastpak brand pack that has a main compartment and a smaller outside compartment. I bought it for backpack fishing in 1983 and it is still going strong over thirty years later. Although I occasionally wish for more compartments to keep things better organized, I really don't need them and, in all honesty, I don't want to slide down the slippery slope to more pockets for more stuff. At that point, I might as well put on my waders, my fully loaded vest, and fish all out.

A basic backpack.

There is nothing wrong with that; it is just not backpack fly fishing.

Incidentally, more and more high end fly-fishing catalogs show a variety of packs that cost significantly more, have lots of compartments for holding rod tubes, a variety of fly boxes, water bottles, etc., and that sometimes even convert from a pack to a fly vest. They seem sort of neat but, once again, they go against the basic philosophy that I pursue: keep it simple.

A creel and antique fly rod and reel.

In some ways, the original pack for fly fishing was a wicker creel, which is essentially a small basket for carrying a fly book or fish that have been caught. Prior to the development of the fishing vest by Lee Wulff in the 1930s, flyfishers typically carried a creel, fly rod and reel, and a book of flies, and not much else. Look at old paintings of flyfishermen of the past, or watch the film *A River Runs Through It*, to see what little equipment earlier fishers often used.

One additional comment about backpacks: I like to sew patches on mine that come from places that we have visited. I find that it makes the pack more individualized and interesting to look at, and I enjoy remembering different trips that we have taken and even memorable bodies of water and fish that I found in them.

ROD AND REEL

I recommend a medium-weight rod and reel combination that will allow you to cast the range of flies that you are carrying. For me, a 5-weight rod has ended up being the best, but a 6- or even 7-weight might work better for you. With the 5-weight, and with the right leader, I am able to cast flies that range from tiny dry flies to small bass poppers or hair bugs.

The brand or price range of rod and reel that you want is really dependent on your personal choice. Fly rods may be reasonably priced, or they can cost more than $800 for a higher-priced graphite rod or around $1,500 for a quality handmade bamboo rod. I use one of several different

A pair of inexpensive fly rods and reels.

rods and reels. One is a two-piece eight-and-a-half-foot graphite rod that I built a couple of years ago, and another is a six-piece eight-foot Cortland rod that fits inside the pack itself. I also own two other eight-foot 5-weight rods (one of which I built) and two heavier rods. If I know that I will probably be fishing, I will take a two-piece rod because it is easier to set up quickly, but if I am unsure if I will be fishing and I am just bringing my pack to be prepared, I will bring the pack rod and reel in my pack. Each of the combinations that I use costs about $200 for the rod, reel, and line—in other words, pretty much low cost, economy level equipment.

As I mentioned in the introduction to this book, I have accumulated several fly rods over the years and, as I turn more and more to backpack fly fishing, I like to alternate them on my fishing trips. My original rod is a 7-weight but, as mentioned above, the majority are 5-weights, and I have found that the 5-weight works well under a variety of conditions for trout, bluegills, and smaller bass. I do own two heavier rods for larger flies, an 8- and a 9-weight, but I only use these if I am fishing with larger wind resistant largemouth bass flies or heavier saltwater streamers.

My original fly rod is fiberglass, but the majority of my fly rods are graphite, which is what you will typically find in a sporting goods store today. (Although a somewhat silly practice, I tend to nickname my fly rods, and my original fly rod ended up being named Trusty.) I do own one split bamboo fly rod that I built, but it is inexpensive as bamboo rods go. All of my fly rods are basic, bare bones tools and all work fine. Sometimes it is fun to fish with a bamboo rod, just because it is more old fashioned and traditional. I remember my father, who was not a fisherman, telling me that my grandfather fly fished in the Catskill Mountains in the years prior to World War II. Sadly, my grandfather's bamboo fly rod did not survive, and he died when I was an infant, so I never had the opportunity to listen to stories of his fishing experiences during those early days. And I would *love* to have seen what fly rod he used and even tried it out.

My overall point here is that you do not need the most expensive fly rod to backpack fly fish. A decent lower-priced fly rod will work fine, or you can use a more expensive rod if that is more to your liking. You do not need one that fits in a backpack, either, although I have come to like having that option for times when we are going for a hike and I don't want to carry a fly rod all day or if we are traveling a long distance by car or plane. So, my recommendations:

1. If you already have a fly rod, use it and have fun!
2. If you already have a fly rod but have the extra money to buy another one that fits into your daypack, it will be a good investment.
3. If you don't have a fly rod and want to get one, I suggest getting one that fits in your pack because it will give you the option of having it ready at all times and available for those times that you are hiking and may or may not fish.
4. Generally, select a fly rod matched to a line weight that will be useful with the widest range of fish that you are most likely to encounter. For trout, panfish, and light bass, a 5- to 7-weight is probably best. If you are focusing on saltwater fish or larger bass, then something heavier, like a 7- to 9-weight, might be in order.

Because a fly reel is primarily a line storage device and is not typically used in fighting a fish, I suggest the least expensive functional reel that works for you. I have reels that generally fall into the $40 to $55 range and are typically the least expensive in their product lines. As with fly rods, you may spend a lot more (hundreds of dollars) on a fly reel if that is important to you, but it is really not necessary for catching fish and having fun.

Fly lines by reputable companies are typically of good quality, and you will pay between $40 and $60. I have found that I rely only on weight-forward floating lines and not on other specialized lines, such as sinking and sink-tip lines. Again, select a line weight that will give you the widest range of options for the type of fishing you are likely to do.

LEADERS

I can deal with the widest range of situations by carrying a variety of leaders. Leaders are rated by size that is listed as their X value. The lower the X number, the heavier the leader, so a 4X leader is a heavier and stronger leader than a 7X leader. Leaders are selected depending on the size of the fly with which you are fishing. I always bring several 4X and 5X leaders for trout, pan fish, small bass, and other warmwater fish. I also carry heavier leaders for casting cork poppers or small bass bugs—say around a 1X to 3X leader. I also carry spools of tippet material to match each of these sizes so that I can lengthen a leader or extend its useful life. I would say that most of my backpack fly fishing is done with a 4X or 5X leader, but I will also go to a finer leader if I find myself on a beautiful little trout stream in the height of summer. So, the overall point is to bring a variety of leaders with you. This is one area where I don't skimp, because leaders get tangled or break off, and you may well need to change them.

People who are used to spin fishing may not be accustomed to thinking in terms of the X number of a leader but instead think of the pound test of their fishing line. Table 4.1 shows the pound test strengths reported on Orvis leaders as of 2014. This will give you a sense of how strong the tip of each leader is. Keep in mind that, like fly lines, leaders have to be matched to the size of the flies

TABLE 4.1

Leader Sizes, Pound Test, and Suggested Fly Sizes (Size and Pound Test Taken from Orvis Leader Packages; Fly Sizes Suggested by the Author)

Leader X Value	Pound Test	Fly Sizes
0	15.5	Larger bass bugs and saltwater streamers
1	13.5	Larger bass bugs and saltwater streamers
2	11.5	Bigger freshwater streamers and other flies: #4–8
3	8.5	Freshwater streamers and other flies: #8–12
4	6	All freshwater flies in sizes #12–16
5	4.75	All freshwater flies in sizes #14–18
6	3.5	All freshwater flies in sizes #18–20
7	2.5	All freshwater flies in sizes #20–22

that are being cast. I have included the fly size ranges for the leader X sizes shown, from my personal experience.

FLIES

The selection of flies can be challenging as you shift your thinking into the backpack fly-fishing philosophy. Many flyfishers are used to carrying as many flies as possible on the outside chance that *one particular fly* is what the fish will want that day. In my fly-fishing vest, for example, I have flies that I vividly recall using on the Housatonic River in Connecticut to fish the white fly hatch with Tom in the early 1980s and that I have never used since. Over time, I found that, if I was going trout fishing, I would carry my vest with every possible fly in it, and I started to develop the same tendency with bass fly fishing.

Not so with backpack fly fishing! With this approach, I take a single fly box that I have loaded with a variety of flies that I am most likely to turn to and in which I have confidence. These are the flies that I absolutely and positively would not leave home without and that might work on the widest variety of fish in the widest variety of situations. Below is a beginning list to give you a flavor of what I use, but keep in mind that your minimalist selection may be different and reflect the waters and fish where you live. We will discuss fly selections and descriptions more in chapter 6.

I should note that, on some occasions, the size and color of a fly matters a great deal, and fish may be very selective in which artificial flies they go after and which ones they don't. This is why trout flyfishers in particular try to "match the hatch" with close imitations, and that is also why they end up with bulging vests full of fly boxes that are full of different patterns. In backpack fly fishing, we do not carry all of those flies and, instead, we do our best with the limited selection that we have in the fly box. In practice, I have rarely found this to be a significant limitation. Instead, I have found that, as long as I carry flies in a variety of sizes, I have been able to have a good shot at catching fish in a wide range of situations. It has always seemed to me that the size of a fly tends to matter more than its color, or even its shape.

Dry Flies. My go-to dry fly is a caddis imitation in a range of sizes from 14 to 20. Many people would prefer an Elk Hair Caddis, but I have always preferred the Henryville Special, which was developed here in the Poconos of Northeast Pennsylvania. A caddis imitation is essential because I have found that, more often than not, I am more likely to encounter caddis flies than mayflies. When trout hit the top with splashy rises, sometimes coming right out of the water, I know to try a caddis imitation. As mentioned earlier, my version of the Henryville Special, the Hairwing Henryville, simply substitutes a small highly visible wing of white synthetic hair in place of the traditional duck quill. I prefer this fly mostly because it is easier for me to tie, lasts longer after catching fish, and can be seen more easily on the water. In addition to a caddis imitation, I bring a couple of mayfly imitations in darker and lighter colors. I like the Adams and the Light Cahill, both in #12 to #18 and that is about it for dry flies. Again, you will only need a few flies in a range of sizes and with a history of some success to give you confidence in them.

Wet Flies. I admit a partiality to traditional wet flies. They have fallen so out of favor that catalogs for major fly-fishing companies often omit them altogether. But they are beautiful and traditional, and they work in a surprisingly wide range of circumstances. You don't need a vast array of them, but maybe three or four different types in #12 or #14. My favorites are the Professor, the Dark Cahill, the Royal Coachman (with red, yellow, or orange floss bodies), and a Partridge and Yellow (or Orange). I also carry the Wilsons' Bully's Bluegill Spider because it really works on warmwater fish. Wet flies stripped in fast work very well on almost any type of water and, depending on the conditions, almost any type of fish. In fact, if I had to be stuck with literally one fly, it might well be a Professor. (But, then again, the Hairwing Henryville fished like a wet fly underwater works great also . . . So, okay *two* flies . . .)

Streamers. I find streamers to be beautiful and like them for the same reasons as wet flies. I like the Grey Ghost, Black Ghost (feather wing and marabou wing), and Mickey Finn in smaller sizes, such as a #12. Although it is newer and I tend to stick with traditional flies, the Beadhead

Wooly Bugger is an amazing fly that truly works. Trout love it, but so do bass, pickerel, perch, and other fish. It just works, so I carry it. Streamers are terrific all-purpose flies that can catch a variety of freshwater and saltwater fish. They are essential if you fish coastal areas for small stripers and bluefish.

Nymphs. I tend to gravitate to three different nymphs: the Pheasant Tail, the Montana Stonefly nymph, and the Hare's Ear. I carry pretty small Pheasant Tails (#16 and #18) and larger Montana's and Hare's Ears. These do a good job of covering a wide set of situations. Sometimes, they come in handy in situations in which you did not expect to use them. For example, a few years ago I caught several nice-sized calico bass off a dock using a small Pheasant Tail nymph fished fast. I am not sure why the crappies went after it, but they did, and it was fun!

Popper and Bass Bugs. I do carry a few Gaines poppers in small bass/bluegill sizes. I prefer to tie my own flies and bass bugs, but I have found that these are very easy to cast with my 5-weight rod, so they fit the bill. I am working on tying a hair bug that will be as small and easy to cast, and I am almost there, so it will soon join the box.

FLY BOX

It would be easy to find yourself deciding to carry *two* fly boxes, or even more. Resist the urge! The fun and challenge is to restrict yourself to one fly box. And that, naturally, leads us to trying to find a fly box with as much storage as possible. Although that is understandable, try to find one that easily carries your selection but is not too large or cumbersome.

The one I primarily use has two sides, one with foam ripples for storing dry flies and the other with eight small compartments for wets, streamers, nymphs, and poppers. It measures 4 inches by 6 inches and is plenty big enough to carry the assortment listed above. This fly box was a gift from my son Brendan many years ago and somehow never quite fit my fly-fishing vest, but it is *perfect* for my backpack. Shop around and find a fly box that will work best for you. On other specific occasions, I might substitute another fly box. For example, when I fished Cape Breton in Nova Scotia for trout recently, I brought my Wheatley fly box that my dad gave me with my first fly-tying kit. In it I only carried wet flies and streamers, because they were all that were needed there to catch fish. It is a beautiful, traditional fly box filled with colorful flies for trout, and I could have fished an entire season in Nova Scotia with that minimal collection of flies.

NIPPERS

I carry a simple nipper, and it is one of only two things that I have attached to the *outside* of my backpack. I have found that rooting around for clippers is aggravating, and I use them often to change flies, add tippet material, etc. The only other thing attached to the outside of my backpack is a fleece patch.

FLEECE PATCH

This is important so that I don't put wet flies back into the box where they, and other flies in the box, will rust.

FLOATANT

I carry a small bottle of floatant gel for dry flies or small bass hair bugs.

LEATHERMAN OR NEEDLE-NOSED PLIERS

I carry my Leatherman tool or a small pair of pliers to crimp down the barbs on the hooks of my flies before I use them and to remove hooks from fish as quickly as possible.

SUNGLASSES

Polarized sunglasses are essential for seeing the details below the surface and for general eye protection.

FIRST AID KIT

I carry a small first aid kit because I am often hiking as well as fishing. It just makes sense to carry some bandages, antibiotic ointment, etc.

SUNSCREEN

I hate the stuff but it is very important, so throw a small tube into your backpack and use it! It will then be there to share with others who have forgotten it. Of course, it makes sense to rinse your hands after using sunscreen so that the scent is not transferred to your flies.

BANDANA

My family thinks that I am crazy because I love bandanas, but they are *so useful*! I have to credit my brother Dave for championing the cause of bandanas. I have often seen Dave with a bandana stuffed in his right-hand pocket to keep his car keys from falling out and for any other purposes that may arise. Bandanas are cheap, colorful, readily available, and incredibly useful. I always carry at least one or more in my backpack, and one in my pocket as I hike. You can stuff one in your pocket to prevent your keys from falling out, you can use them to wipe the sweat off your brow, and they are great for cleaning off your hands after landing and releasing a fish. I think that I own about twelve to fourteen, and I could always use more. And they are cheap, so there is no excuse to not own a bunch.

There are so many uses for bandanas that I have encountered over the years, but Table 4.2 lists twenty to make the case for bandanas. If you don't have any, I suggest that you go out and buy at least five—you won't regret it!

LICENSE

Okay, so there is a third item attached to the outside of my backpack: my fishing license. I was talking about the idea for this book with a friend who is not a fisher but is a serious AT (Appalachian Trail) hiker, and he asked (in all innocence), "Don't you need a license or something?" Great question, and the answer is *yes!* So,

TABLE 4.2
Twenty Possible Uses for Bandanas

1. To keep your car keys from falling out of your pocket while hiking.
2. To wipe your hands off after hand-landinga fish that you have caught.
3. For wiping off blood from superficial wounds and cuts.
4. To wrap, pad, and protect cameras, reels, and other items in your backpack.
5. To wipe off fogged up eye glasses.
6. To serve as a place mat for a sandwich or apple on the forest floor at lunchtime.
7. To use as a general-use napkin during meals in the woods.
8. To use as a headscarf.
9. To wipe sweat off your neck or forehead.
10. To dry off a fly rod before putting it away in its tube.
11. For blowing or wiping your nose, particularly during allergy season.
12. To use as a "place mat" for your wallet and keys on a dresser top in an unfamiliar cabin, so that you always know where they are when you wake up.
13. To wrap around your wallet and keys before putting them in a storage pouch in your tent at nighttime.
14. To dry the inside floor of a damp tent.
15. To dry off picnic table tops and benches.
16. To tie to a tree branch or shrub to mark your return path at a tricky fork in a hiking trail.
17. To dry your feet after wet wading before putting your hiking socks and shoes back on.
18. To use as a temporary bandage for a more serious wound.
19. To dry off the wet seat of a canoe.
20. To wipe away a tear if the fish won't bite!

wherever your backpacking journeys take you, buy a license first. They do cost money, but then the proceeds are used to protect the environment and fishing. I save old licenses as souvenirs of past trips, and they are great to pull out and look at on a snowy day deep in the winter.

SOME OPTIONAL EQUIPMENT

I have started carrying binoculars because a variety of really interesting birds live near water, including kingfishers, osprey, a variety of ducks, cedar waxwings, and bald eagles. They, and many other birds, are beautiful and fascinating, and many a slow fishing day has been improved with seeing one of these.

Great blue heron.

I have also found binoculars useful in identifying turtles and other wildlife near and around water. Some birds are incredible fishers, and their behavior can give us clues about where fish are. Look for bald eagles and ospreys, kingfishers, mergansers, herons, and egrets, all of which are master fishers. Near salt water, look for seagulls, terns, and cormorants.

Although it is not essential, I carry a small digital camera for photographing fish, streams and rivers, ponds and lakes, birds, wildflowers, and other wildlife. The development of small digital cameras has opened the door

Another master fisherman: cormorant.

An osprey scans the water for fish.

to so many possibilities for capturing the beautiful places that we encounter and the fish and wildlife that live there. Most of the photographs included in this book were taken with small digital cameras. We will discuss the importance of photography more in chapter 6.

I like to carry a measuring tape to measure all of the fish that I reasonably can. (If a fish is in distress or I can't easily control it to measure it, I just let it go). A big part of the fun of fishing is keeping records of all fish that I have caught and their sizes. Because I have never found a reliable measure of weight that would work on a live fish, measuring the length of fish seems to be the best approach. The tape measure that I carry is a small roll of nylon that won't rust. If you don't care about measuring the fish you catch, then this item is dispensable.

Finally, I occasionally put a pair of wading sandals in my backpack if I anticipate getting wet along a rocky stream. However, most of the time I don't have these with me because they are not essential and they take up room in my backpack.

What You Will Not Need

As I stated earlier in this book, backpack fly fishing is not the only way to fish. So, if you like using any of the following equipment (as I sometimes do), by all means do so . . . but you will not need them when backpack fly fishing!

- Fly-fishing vest
- Multiple fly boxes
- Waders
- Landing net
- Wading staff

Stick with the minimum that will fit in a small day-pack. Here is a photo of my pack with all of the equipment that I typically use taken out. (As mentioned above, the wading sandals are usually omitted.) As you can see, I can fit quite a bit into it, and I have found that these are all that I need.

Summary

If you like to travel light to begin with, then it is not hard to narrow down what you need for backpack fly fishing. But if you are used to heading out with a fully loaded fly vest and waders, then you will need to adjust your think-

Backpack contents.

ing somewhat. As I have noted here, you really don't need a lot. In fact, I could cut my fly collection in my single box by half and still do well out on a stream or pond. Just carry the basics of what you need, leave your backpack where it is ready to go, and then grab it whenever you head out. You never know when a short hike will lead to some great fishing, but if you are not ready, you will find yourself coming upon a *fishy* looking body of water, and then you will wish you had brought your backpack. Trust me . . . I have done it too many times!

Chapter Five

It Works!
Examples of Backpack Fly Fishing in Action

Over the past thirty-five years or so, I have had the opportunity to fish in a number of different waters for different species using only the simple equipment described earlier in this book. In this chapter, I will describe several of these experiences in order to illustrate that the backpack fly-fishing method can be quite successful in a wide range of situations. Naturally, these experiences may be rather different from yours, and you will accumulate (or have already done so) your own set of memories to look back on. The experiences that I describe here mostly involve freshwater fishing, with a focus on coldwater environments for trout and warmwater environments for bass, panfish, and other species.

As we progress through this chapter, we will take a closer look at how we can apply the five-step ASCAL (Approach, Select, Cast, Animate, Land) method to a several different examples. I have organized these examples by the type of water (cold fresh water, warm fresh water, salt water) that the fish live in. As discussed in the previous chapters, the essence of backpack fly fishing is to use the simple equipment that we are carrying to respond to the demands of various situations. We make creative adaptations, not through varied and complicated equipment, but in *how* we complete the five steps in each different situation.

In the first example, I have spelled out how each step of the ASCAL method was implemented. I did not do so for the remaining examples to avoid repetition. Instead, for the remaining examples, the implementation of the ASCAL method is embedded in the description of the body of water and how I fished it. At this point, I assume that you have become familiar with the steps of the ASCAL method and can identify any unique issue that arose from my descriptions.

Cold Freshwater Fishing

Coldwater streams, rivers, and ponds typically hold trout, and they can be beautiful places that lend themselves naturally to backpack fly fishing. Here are a few examples of some of these amazing environments and how I tried to use the backpack fly-fishing approach to reveal their secrets.

STERLING POND, VERMONT

Sterling Pond is a lovely alpine lake located near Smuggler's Notch in the Green Mountains of Vermont at about three thousand feet above sea level. I was fortunate enough to

Sterling Pond, Vermont.

hike up to the pond again recently with my family, almost thirteen years to the day since we had last made the ascent. The hike up to the pond is not long in distance (just a bit over a mile), but the majority of the path is up a steep flight of irregular rock "stairs" through a mixed hardwood and evergreen forest. It is a strenuous hike up with a gain in altitude of one thousand feet, and not one on which you would want to carry lots of fishing equipment. In other words, it is a perfect place to try some backpack fly fishing.

Approach: When we reached the top of the path that leads up to the pond from the parking area below, I saw that the trail sloped gently down to the shore of the pond. My first glimpse of the pond through the trees revealed a smallish body of water lined closely with pines and other evergreen trees. There are no houses or other signs of civilization that border the pond, so it is a secluded and beautiful place to fish. As we walked down the gently sloping gravel path toward the shore, I spotted the large granite boulder that provides one of the few open areas from which to cast and where I had caught a brook trout thirteen years earlier. On this day, however, a group of young college-aged men and women had gotten there first and were using the boulder to picnic and swim in the pond. They were laughing, jumping into the lake, making a lot of noise, and generally having fun. It was clearly not the place for me to stop and fish, so we continued down the path as it wound its way along the western and then northern shore of the pond. The path proceeded up a steep flight of wooden stairs and back into the woods. A few hundred yards from the first boulder area, a second set of stairs led down to a small opening in the trees along the shore of the pond. This looked to be the last decent place to try for fishing, so we headed down. A boulder provided an area for my family to relax and rest while I assembled my six-piece fly rod and took out my fly box from my backpack.

Fly Selection: As I scanned the pond for clues, a few things were fairly obvious. First, the pond curved down around a bend and to the right, so there was clearly a lot of pond that I would not be able to access. Second, there was little to no vegetation on the water, such as lily pads, and the water was extremely cold to the touch. These clues, along with its altitude in the Green Mountains and my own past experience, let me know that I was likely to find trout here, brook trout specifically, due to their preference for cold and pristine habitats. There was a light breeze, and I also noted that there was no surface insect activity and no signs of fish hitting the top. A high, alpine pond such as this typically is not rich in insect life, and fish must be opportunists who will take advantage of any sources of food, including other smaller fish, to survive the harsh winters—so a streamer was a good place to start. I checked my fly box and noted that I only had five or six streamers. I decided to go with a Dark Spruce streamer, a pretty streamer fly with dark brown feather wings and a body of red floss and green, iridescent peacock herl. The overall dark brown color matched the tea-colored water of the pond so it seemed only appropriate.

Cast: My back-cast area was extremely limited due to the trees that lined the pond, even in this more open area. Also, with the cold water and drop off near the shore, wet wading into the pond would be limited at best. My best bet was to step onto a rock that was furthest out in the pond (a foot or two from the shore) and cast to my left, parallel to the shoreline. This would allow me to cover at least the length of my cast back to my spot. I also tried some roll casts directly in front of me and to my right, but these were somewhat short and did not allow me to cover much water, particularly in light of the increasing wind. I concentrated my efforts on a sidearm cast to my left along the shore, and I knew that I would have limited chances to catch something before my family was ready to start the hike back down, particularly as the rainstorms of the morning were showing signs of worsening again.

Animation: As discussed in chapter 2, one of the things that I like best about streamers is the active way that you can retrieve them with good effect. I cast the Dark Spruce off to my left, using a sidearm cast, and then retrieved it using short, irregular pulls on the fly line with my left (line retrieval) hand. As the fly approached me, I watched it carefully through the tea-colored water to see how it looked swimming through the water and to watch behind it for a following fish.

Landing: On the third or fourth cast, I felt a slight tug on the fly, and then nothing. I stripped the fly in toward me again and noted that it was intact. The pull on it could have come from it hitting a rock or a submerged weed, but it also could have been a trout biting at the wing of the fly without making contact with the hook. I immediately cast again to the same spot, or as near to it as possible, and began my retrieve. This time, the tug was immediate and continued as I pulled in the fish. It was a beautiful, 8-inch brook trout, as gorgeous as the pond where it lived. I wet my hand and carefully removed the barbless hook from its mouth. My son Zach took a quick photo with his smart phone and then I released the trout back into its home waters.

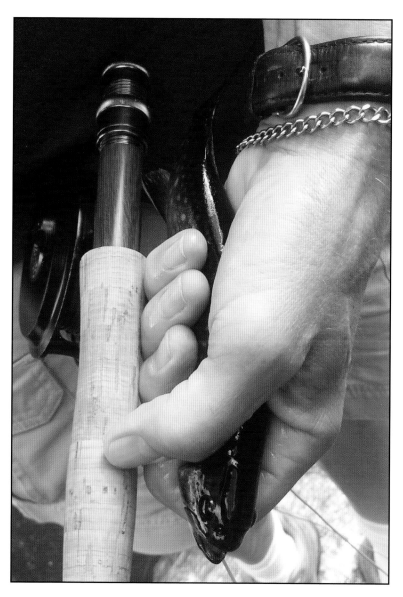

Sterling Pond brook trout.

CAPE BRETON HIGHLANDS NATIONAL PARK, NOVA SCOTIA, CANADA

This unique, rugged, challenging, and beautiful place first inspired my commitment to backpack fly fishing, and it is still draws me again and again. Over the past thirty years, Kathy and I have made the long trek north to Cape Breton, first before we had children, and most recently on our sixth trip with our older son Zach as principle photographer. Cape Breton Highlands National Park is a land of contrasts. The ocean meets the edges of the highlands, and small fresh water streams flow directly into the sea. French speaking Acadians live side by side with people of Scottish ancestry, and names like Cheticamp and Grand

Cabot Trail, Cape Breton Highlands National Park.

Anse contrast with those such as McIntosh Brook and Mackenzie River.

The weather is a constant source of change and contrast, and a cloudless blue-sky day can end in fog and driving rain with little warning. It is a land of northern flora and fauna, where hundred-year-old stunted black spruce survive the harsh winds and winters, and where moose feed in the ponds and then disappear into the misty interior highlands. The highlands hold snowshoe hare, grouse, and secretive lynx. Trees include eastern larch, different types of birch, black spruce, and, in one spot, sugar maples close to three hundred years old. Pilot whales and other whale species are seen from highland overlooks. Speckled trout (as brook trout are called in Canada) inhabit the

Highland mists.

tea-colored waters of the streams, rivers, and ponds, while fall and spring runs of Atlantic salmon still enter their ancestral waters for spawning.

The park is located on Cape Breton Island, which forms the northeastern end of Nova Scotia. Nova Scotia is shaped much like a lobster that stretches from its tail in the southwest to its claws in the northeast. Cape Breton Island forms the claws, and at the top of the left-hand claw is where you will find Cape Breton Highlands National Park. The Cabot Trail, one of the most scenic roads in North America, circumnavigates the western, northern, and eastern boundaries of the park, from Cheticamp in the western end to Ingonish on the eastern entrance. The interior of the park is accessible only by selected trails, and most of it remains a mystery to visitors, with names on the

A Cape Breton moose feeds in a highland lake.

Cheticamp River.

map such as Everlasting Barrens. (If that name doesn't fire your imagination, nothing will!) The rugged highlands, often shrouded in mists, are a clear reminder of why this land is called New Scotland.

On our most recent trip, we drove for two and a half long days from our home in Pennsylvania to get to the park. Once in Nova Scotia, we passed over the Canso Causeway to Cape Breton Island, then wound our way north, passing through First Nation towns of Wagmatcook and Wycomagh, villages of the native MicMac (Mi'kmaq) people. When we finally arrived at the park, we set up tents in the Cheticamp campground outside the town of Cheticamp and within the park boundaries. The Acadian flag of blue, white, and red vertical bars with a gold star on the blue field flew everywhere, celebrating with pride the Acadian culture. (Some ancestors of these people, who were forced out by the British during the French and Indian War, ended up in Louisiana, where the word *Acadian* morphed into the term *Cajun*.) After setting up camp, I bought my park licenses and we were ready to try fishing the beautiful waters of the park.

Corney Brook

This beautiful woodland stream, like others in the park, starts in the highlands and then flows west until it empties

Bridge over Corney Brook.

directly into the ocean. A hiking trail follows the stream from the Cabot Trail into the interior and then ends at a scenic waterfall. The water in Corney Brook, like all the other streams and ponds, is stained deep brown by the tannic acids of the trees so that it looks as if well-steeped tea flowed through the forest undergrowth.

Speckled trout live here and, in this harsh environment, they rarely reach large sizes, with a fish of 8 inches being fairly large. (My personal best for the park is 8.25 inches. The smallest is perhaps 4.5 inches.) These trout are not large, but they are among the most beautiful of all fish that I have encountered. I use traditional wet flies here, exclusively: the Professor, Royal Coachman (red and yellow bodies), Dark Cahill, and Iron Blue Dun.

Traditional brook trout flies.

To use the ASCAL method on Corney Brook (or any water in the park), I hike the trail by the stream and look for small pools that might hold trout and that would allow even a short sidearm or roll cast. (Trees and shrubs can make this very difficult.) Because trout face upstream as they fight the current and wait for food, it is always best to approach pools from the bottom whenever possible and to keep a low profile. I select flies based mostly on my personal preference and mood, as any wet fly may be successful, because these fish are opportunists and cannot be highly selective. I use whatever cast will get a fly on the water, hopefully near the head of a pool, where water enters from the stream

Speckled trout from Corney Brook.

above. I then animate the fly with quick strips, referred to as "panic strips." Trout, entirely hidden by the tea-colored water, emerge to rise to the fly as it escapes. Watching these beautiful fish rise to a traditional wet fly is as exciting as watching a wary and selective trout rise to a dry fly.

Further down the path, by the Corney Brook campground overlooking the ocean, Corney Brook empties its waters directly into the Gulf of St. Lawrence. The last pool before it enters the ocean is perhaps the most unusual trout pool that I have ever encountered. It is literally within a stone's throw of the ocean water, and yet it harbors speckled trout—truly a boundary between the freshwater and saltwater worlds. I fished it by casting a wet fly into the very top of the pool where the water from upstream

The "Ocean Pool."

entered this last deep pool before spilling into the ocean. Again, I used a fast retrieve to animate the fly. Trout were waiting there, as I had remembered from past trips.

After returning home from our most recent trip to the park, I spent part of an afternoon reviewing some of the excellent photographs that my son Zach had taken for this book. I came to the photos of the two trout that I caught on Corney Brook that day, one about two miles inland on our hike, and the other in this ocean-side pool at the mouth of the brook. At the time that I caught the fish, I was not looking for the obvious differences in the fish that the photographs show, yet my later review of the pictures showed them clearly. Notice the differences: the brook (speckled) trout caught further inland and shown in chapter 3 has the expected coloration and shape, with the dark green vertical bands, the orange belly, the white throat, and the orange and white edged fins—in other words, a typical gorgeous brook trout. The fish caught in the ocean-side pool, shown on the following page, has a more muted coloration, overall greyish, but still with the spots of a brook trout. Also, on careful inspection, it is clear that its head is proportionally smaller than the first trout. This presented an intriguing naturalist's mystery to me: why the difference between these two brook trout, caught in the same river, roughly two miles apart on the same day?

I went to my library of books on different types of fish and the answer became obvious. Peter Thompson's terrific book *The Game Fishes of New England and Southeastern Canada* provided the answer. The second fish was a sea

Sea run brook trout.

run brook trout, sometimes referred to as a "salter." These fascinating fish are freshwater trout that take on the behavior and life cycle of anadromous fish, such as Atlantic salmon or American shad that live in salt water and return to their natal fresh water rivers to spawn. Sea run brook trout enter salt water but stay near shore, often in the estuaries of their home rivers. According to Thompson, when they re-enter rivers to spawn, their color reverts to its typical shades and hues.

This event points out one of the real advantages of backpack fly fishing. Using this approach, I try to open my mind to the possibilities that might present themselves as I fish new bodies of water. That day, I was not planning on catching a new type of fish and, quite honestly, I was not even aware that those fish lived there. I simply was hiking, exploring, and fishing. Catching a sea run brook trout was a wonderful surprise and a bonus for the day. Additionally, the ability to photograph fish that I catch whenever possible allows me to look for subtle differences that may not be evident when I catch a fish and then try to release it as quickly as possible without injury. We will discuss this aspect of backpack fly fishing in greater detail in chapter 6.

McIntosh Brook

McIntosh Brook flows north from the central northern edge of the park into the Grand Anse River, which then

The pool on McIntosh Brook.

flows west to the Gulf of St. Lawrence. It is a bit smaller than Corney Brook but is similar in look and in the tactics used to fish it.

Casting into the waterfall pool.

McIntosh Brook trout.

As with Corney Brook, a beautiful woodland path follows the stream up to a waterfall. The pool at the base of this waterfall was where I first caught trout here, over thirty years ago, and it is still one of my favorite places on earth. There is nothing more fun than casting a wet fly into the pool right where the water falls into it from the waterfall above, and then stripping the fly across the pool in short, rapid pulls. Watch the trout rise from the depths of the tea-colored water in the pool . . . there he is . . . here he comes . . . got him!

Cheticamp River

The Cheticamp River is much larger and wilder than the streams described previously. The Cheticamp is an Atlantic

The wild Cheticamp River.

salmon river, and my only explorations of fishing for these elusive and fascinating fish have occurred on the Cheticamp. (Actually, I did once fish the Apsy River, another of the park's salmon rivers, while camping years ago. I caught a number of what I thought were feisty small brook trout. Wrong! These were salmon fry, living in the stream until they could grow into smolt and make their way back to the Atlantic Ocean. I quickly learned my mistake and left them alone!) The Salmon Hole Trail begins at the Cheticamp campground and follows the river in for about four miles, passing four salmon pools: First Pool, Chance Pool, Second Pool, and Third Pool. Again, the water is tea-colored, but the river is wilder, wider, and a bit intimidating. Winds can swirl out from the interior of the highlands, making casting difficult.

I have fished the Cheticamp each time I have visited the park, but never for long, because I am always with my family and we are there to hike as well as fish. So, my experience as a salmon fisherman is almost nonexistent, compared to those who make week-long pilgrimages to the rivers of Quebec, New Brunswick, or Nova Scotia each year, fishing from dawn to dusk with the support of paid guides. Typically, I catch no salmon, but I may be lucky to catch another speckled trout. Once I caught a 12-inch salmon smolt, and on another time I caught a 21-inch grilse, or first year returning salmon. Considering how short my windows of opportunity have been, I consider myself more than lucky to have done so. I always carry a small supply of salmon flies on our trips to the park, which I use nowhere else, and I have always ended up using a traditional Mickey

Fishing the First Pool on the Cheticamp.

Finn streamer that a local fisherman once recommended to me. Salmon are fascinating fish, and their tremendous decline is a tragedy of our time. I fear that there may come a time when their returns to the rivers will be too weak to warrant fishing for them. I feel incredibly fortunate to have caught one and seen it firsthand.

Cape Breton Highlands National Park and Backpack Fly Fishing

The streams and rivers that I have just described are best accessed and fished while hiking with a simple backpack, a fly rod, and a box of flies. It is the quintessential backpack fly-fishing environment. During recent trips to the park, I have seen fishermen wearing the full fly-fishing regalia: featherweight waders with wading shoes and gravel cuffs, wading belts, landing nets, bulging fly vests, and top of the line fly rods and reels. Quite frankly, they looked ridiculously out of place in that environment, and their equipment was more than overkill. Little of it was necessary. Although it is clearly someone's choice to use whatever equipment he or she enjoys, I urge people who visit this vast and lovely land to travel lightly and simply and enjoy the wildlife that live there.

HICKORY RUN STATE PARK, PENNSYLVANIA

Hickory Run State Park, located near my home in the Poconos region of eastern Pennsylvania, is a beautiful natural environment that offers a number of outdoor recreational activities, including hiking, camping, swimming, hunting (in certain areas), and fishing. The park is home to a wide variety of eastern wildlife, notably black bear. (Some of the largest black bear in the United States come from the Pocono region of Pennsylvania.) A central feature of the park is the Boulder Field, an expanse of boulders and stones the size of a small lake located within an otherwise forested area. The park literature explains that the boulder field is the result of ancient glacier activity in the region, and today it is a striking and mysterious natural feature of the park. For a backpack flyfisher, Hickory Run State Park is characterized by small to medium trout streams lined with hemlock trees and thick stands of wild rhododendron. The streams hold stocked brown trout and some wild brown and brook trout. Of these streams, three have been of particular interest to me.

Sand Spring Run

One of the most beautiful hiking trails in the park is the Shades of Death Trail. The trail was named by early set-

Sand Spring Run flows through the wild rhododendron.

tlers in the area, who found the rocky and heavily forested environment harsh and unwelcoming. The hike follows Sand Spring Run, a small forest stream that is segmented by remnants of dams from the 1800s. The hike is heavily forested, and the intertwined root systems on the path pose a tripping hazard for hikers who are not careful. The stream is fast and characterized by long stretches of riffles, punctuated by occasional small pools. Even fishable pools are often difficult to access due to overhanging tree branches, thick shrubbery, and underbrush, and dapping or simply dropping a fly on an open space is sometimes the only way to fish these areas. Areas above the dam remnants offer the best chance for casting along the length of the hike, but even the unfishable areas are beautiful. This stream is a natural environment for backpack fly fishing.

Recently, Kathy, Zach, and I hiked the stream on a warm August day. We spotted good-sized trout in one fairly open pool, but they were so wary that my first cast put them down on both occasions, and my use of the AS-CAL method failed, not with the Approach step, but with the Cast step. I am still not sure *how* to cast to these trout without alarming them, and this presents a challenge to puzzle out for a future trip. The area above the most intact of the remaining dam remnants is backed up enough to form a pond-like expanse of water. As the stream enters this slow section, small native brook trout are evident, but they are in one of the heavily overgrown areas and casting is impossible. I tried the dapping method, and the fish were curious but extremely wary and not to be fooled.

Brown trout.

At Zach's urging, I also tried the slow area from atop the dam itself, casting a traditional Dark Cahill wet fly to a pod of brown trout that were cruising the lake-like area. I cast to these fish as they cruised near the dam and then stripped the fly in rapidly, catching one 11-inch brown and interesting another that followed the fly but turned off at the last moment. It was amazing to watch the fish follow the "fleeing" fly and rise to attack it from below. The color of these fish, with their tan flanks, red spots, and yellow bellies, is a fascinating contrast to the color of wild brook trout. Sand Spring Run is one of those small eastern woodland brooks that sometimes looks too little to hold fish but then surprises you if you look hard enough for holding spots. The holdover brook trout, in particular, are hardy survivors, small but wary, and perfectly adapted to this kind of environment.

Mud Run

Mud Run is clearly a misnamed stream. It is a beautiful woodland stream, lined with thick stands of hemlock trees and wild rhododendron.

Larger than Sand Spring Run, Mud Run is a medium stream with more clearly defined pools and fishable riffles. According to local books on trout streams of the area, Mud Run's temperature remains more constant than other area streams because of the shading protection of the overhanging trees and shrubbery that line its banks. The area that I fish is reached by a popular trail that leads to a small waterfall where a smaller brook enters Mud Run. One area that I have fished with success is where a series of riffles flow around some boulders and rocks in the stream

Mud Run.

and then enter a long, slow, deeper pool. The stream flows from left to right, and an open area of gravel sandbar keeps the trees and vegetation back from the stream edge a bit more, so casting for a right-handed caster is relatively easy. Each time I have fished with success here, I have used small caddis dry fly imitations, because caddis are the most consistent fly that I have observed year round on Pocono trout streams. One time a few years ago, I tied on a small (about a #16) Goddard Caddis and let it drift downstream from the end of the riffle area into the top of the slow pool, without actually casting. An upstream-facing brown trout rose and inhaled the fly on the first drift. More recently, I cast into the riffle area with a #18 Hairwing Henryville Special. The water here is more rapid and less smooth, and trout have less of a chance to inspect flies that pass over them than they do in the slower pool. A trout went after my fly on one of the first casts, but I did not hook it. On the next cast, I was successful in catching a beautiful 7-inch brown trout.

It is important to note that the fish I caught on Mud Run and Sand Spring Run were caught in July and August, at the height of the Pocono summer. Most books on trout fishing in this area provide fly hatch charts that seem to indicate that it is not even worth fishing in July and August due to the heat and the comparative lack of insect life, particularly mayfly hatches. However, like other flyfishers, I have found that the best times to fish are when opportunities to do so present themselves. The point, of course, is keep your backpack ready and fish whenever you can.

Fourth Run

I did not catch anything on this small brook, but Kathy and I saw something amazing here. The hike was long and hot on a July afternoon, winding downhill through the forest to meet the small brook in the underbrush. At first, the brook is so small that it is not even evident that it *is* a brook, but gradually water from the ground seeps into it until it becomes a definable stream. Where we ended our hike, the stream was small enough that you could just about straddle it, although your feet might get a bit wet. According to the park brochure, a stand of blueberry bushes was a reported favorite of black bears, so we kept a wary eye out. Kathy spotted the fish and pointed them out to me: a school of brook trout, all in the 2- to 3-inch range, all facing into the meager current as trout do. These fish were too small to even fish for, but they were fascinating and provided evidence of the incredible ability to survive that these fish possess.

YELLOWSTONE NATIONAL PARK, MONTANA AND WYOMING

Along with Cape Breton Highlands National Park, Yellowstone National Park is one of the most incredible places on earth. We were fortunate enough to live in Billings, Montana, for two years, so we had multiple opportunities to cross over the Beartooth Highway and visit the park. Huge herds of bison, elk, grizzly bears, and wolves live in one of the last wilderness areas accessible to a wide range of people. The geysers, mudpots, deep thermal pools, and

Yellowstone National Park view.

Yellowstone elk.

other geologic phenomena are almost unreal, and it is easy to understand why early explorers to the area were awed and amazed by what they encountered.

Yellowstone National Park is home to several world-famous rivers that are fished heavily every year, including the Yellowstone River, the Madison, the Firehole, and the Gibbon. Using full fly-fishing gear, I have fished several of these—in particular Yellowstone Lake for its large cut-throat trout. However, I also used the backpack fly-fishing approach, as described below.

Yellowstone River

As mentioned in chapter 1, on one hike down to the Yellowstone River, I had the opportunity to use the backpack fly-fishing strategy to good advantage. The path that we took is no longer open to the public, so I feel fortunate to have experienced it and the fishing that it led to. The hike in question involved a steep descent down to the Yellowstone River, about a half-mile in length, with switchbacks to make the trail passable. At that point, I did not own many fly rods, and I put my original two-piece, seven-foot, 7-weight fiberglass fly rod into my backpack. Needless to say, it stuck up out of the top of the backpack quite a bit and I had to duck down in many places so as not to catch it on overhanging branches. The short trail ended at the Yellowstone River. The river here was strong and wild and, even if I had had waders with me, there was no way I would have entered that powerful flow of water. For the moment, I thought I was stymied and, after looking around a bit,

The Yellowstone River.

decided that we should start the strenuous hike back up the way we had come. Then I noticed the small, protected eddy right at my feet, no longer than three feet long and perhaps two feet wide.

The eddy was created by a boulder at the river's edge, and the water, although not by any means still or placid, was slower than the main stem of the current. I could not see the bottom through the stained and roily water, but I thought I saw flashes of white at irregular intervals. Could these be fins, or the opening of a fish's mouth? I decided to investigate, so I tied on a Dark Spruce streamer, mostly because I like the fly pattern and its dark brown color matched that of the water in the eddy. I flipped the fly to the top of the eddy and animated it through the small area with quick wiggles and twitches of the fly rod tip. On my second or third flip, a Yellowstone cutthroat trout, 14 inches in length, grabbed the fly, and I was able to land and measure it. What a beautiful fish! And, this eddy was the only real fishing option at the end of the hike. My experience reinforced in my mind that fish can often be found in areas that are easy to overlook.

As a footnote on this experience, we made the hike back up to the top and, upon arriving at the trailhead, I noticed that the rod's tip section was missing from my pack. Now, I am incredibly loyal to this fly rod in particular, so I made the hike back down by myself to the river, where I found the rod section next to the eddy. The long hike back up a second time was a natural consequence of my failure to carefully pack up my equipment before leaving a fishing area. I will not forget this experience, and it comes back to me every time I check and recheck that I have everything before hiking back to our car or campsite on different hikes.

Gibbon River

One year when we lived in Montana, we met my brother-in-law and his wife at the Norris campground to camp for several days. They had made the trek west from New Jersey to visit us and other friends and to witness a particular meteor shower that was reported to be observable from the park. The Gibbon at this area winds through a meadow by the campground, and its deep undercut banks hold brook trout. Sometimes, bison frequent this area as well. The river here is an easy walk from the campground, so I was able to go make a few quick casts before heading off for the day's hikes and activities. There is little to no tree or shrub cover along the banks of the winding meadow river, so a low and slow approach is essential to not spook the trout. I found that, most of the time, the trout had positioned themselves in the cover of undercut banks where the overhanging stream bank provided protections from predators. I used Pale Morning Dun dry flies, cast to the top of each pool or segment of the stream above the trout, and then dead drifted to where the trout lay under the undercut bank. The trout were small (my records list several 6-inch fish, a 5-inch fish, and one as small as 2.5 inches) but fun and beautiful. It was particularly fun to go down and fish during the evening, with bats circling the stream area and fish rising and jumping as they pursued evening mayflies.

ROSE RIVER, SHENADOAH NATIONAL PARK, VIRGINIA

My family and I met my brother Dave's family for a camping trip when we first moved back to Pennsylvania after two years in Montana. We camped and took many fun hikes in this beautiful park, but my favorite was on the Dark Hollow Falls trail along a branch of the Rose River. At the time, I was just beginning to develop my thoughts about backpack fly fishing, and I brought Trusty and a box of flies in my backpack. We hiked the pretty trail on a warm May day, and when we stopped by one likely looking pool, I selected a Light Cahill dry fly and cast to the head of the pool so that the fly drifted down to where the fish were likely waiting. I caught four wild brook trout, all between 5 and 7 inches long, during the short time that our group wanted to pause and rest. Once again, this is an example of backpack fly fishing within the context of another activity: there were seven people in our group, and we were hiking together, *not* going on a fishing trip. By carrying my fly rod and backpack, I was ready to take advantage of a fifteen-minute rest stop along our hiking trail.

Warm Freshwater Fishing

Beauty comes in different forms, and I never cease to be amazed at the differences between environments such as a woodland trout brook and a mist-covered bass pond in the early morning light. As mentioned previously, flyfishers have historically ranked coldwater fish, such as trout and salmon, as superior in beauty and challenge to warm-

Little green heron and a turtle share a stump in a swampy pond.

water fish. A review of older books on flies for fishing (for example, Mary Orvis Marbury's book, *Favorite Flies and Their Histories*) show that, historically, almost all flies were designed for trout or salmon, with few designed for bass. Those that were designed for bass were essentially over-sized trout flies. Relatively little attention was paid to fishing for bass and other warmwater fish, although the fish were available and certainly challenging and fun to pursue and catch. However, with the pioneering work of Dave Whitlock and others, the end of the twentieth century opened new doors for flyfishers and opened our eyes to the numerous opportunities that warmwater fishing brings.

My first fly-fishing experiences involved fishing for bluegills and other sunfish. Later, I turned my attention to trout, almost to the exclusion of other fish. However, once

I discovered that flies and tactics had been developed for largemouth and smallmouth bass, along with other fish species, I began a consuming interest in that form of fly fishing. I am currently on a quest to catch a really large largemouth bass on a fly, and also a really big pickerel. I would also like to beat my personal best catches of bluegills and calico bass. So, although my earliest experiences with backpack fly fishing were on trout streams, increasingly I have used this approach on ponds and lakes with great enjoyment.

GOULDSBORO LAKE, PENNSYLVANIA

Of all places that I have fished for largemouth bass, calico bass (crappies), pickerel, and sunfish, Gouldsboro Lake has been among my favorite. Located on the Pocono

Promising area on Gouldsboro Lake.

plateau within an hour's drive of my home, this lake is part of a state park system of Tobyhanna and Gouldsboro State Parks. Although I have fished the lake from my canoe with Kathy (including once when she spotted a river otter), I have also fished from the shore with my 5-weight rod and backpack.

Gouldsboro Lake is a moderate-sized lake of about 250 acres, with its southern, more shallow end comprising small islands, coves, and tree stumps. The main lake is open and bordered on three sides by the park property and a railway line. The northern end is bordered by a few houses. The area that I have fished is a cove on the western side where the parking lot, boat launch, accessible fishing pier, and swimming beach are located.

When I fish here, I do so with no preconceived notions as to what I might catch. I fish the weedy areas along the shoreline of the cove using a searching fly pattern such

A Gouldsboro Lake sunfish.

as a small cork bass popper, a traditional wet fly, a small streamer, or a Bully's Bluegill Spider. I have found the Bluegill Spider pattern to be quite successful on a range of fish, including bluegills, calico bass, and largemouth bass. On one occasion, I fished from the pier when no one else was around and caught several calico bass in succession on a Bluegill Spider, stripped in fairly quickly and irregularly. As mentioned earlier, I once caught a bluegill, calico bass, and a nice-sized largemouth bass on the same Bluegill Spider, not quite on consecutive casts but close to each other. At other times, I have been less successful, but I always spot some wildlife: turtles, water snakes, osprey fishing over the main lake, and birds such as orioles and cedar waxwings in the tree canopy along the shore. One of the reasons that I like this lake and others like it is that the shoreline is open for casting, with little to impede my back casts. And, as with so many other bodies of water that I fish in this way, I find myself looking to the areas that are accessible only by canoe or boat and starting to make plans for other fishing trips.

Pickerel caught on a streamer.

MAUCH CHUNK LAKE, PENNSYLVANIA

Mauch Chunk Lake is one of my favorite bass lakes near my home. It is a man-made lake created by a dam on the Mauch Chunk Creek. Although I have mostly fished it from my canoe with Kathy or Tom, and although I often spin fish here, I have also used my fly rod and a handful of bass bugs that I have tied.

My usual bass bug is made of deer hair, spun onto the hook, and then clipped short into a bass bug shape, typically in orange, black, and white. These bass bugs do create more wind resistance that makes casting a bit more dif-

Bassy looking area on Mauch Chunk Lake.

Dragonflies on a lily pad flower bud (above) and a turtle sunning (below).

ficult, so I have continually tried to reduce their size and bulk. I have also used commercially available Gaines cork poppers in small sizes. The bass that I have caught using both of these types of bass bugs have not been large and have ranged from 13 to 16 inches. Recently, I caught a bass of about 13 inches on my hair bug, retrieved slowly and irregularly. The bass first showed itself by the "nervous water" right behind the slowly retrieved bug as it stalked its prey prior to striking. This is an amazing sight, time after time.

The shallow end of the lake is where I prefer to fish. The water here is about five to six feet deep, and there are thick stands of lily pads and other aquatic plants as

A bass fights on top.

you proceed up to the top of the lake where the Mauch Chunk Creek feeds the lake. There is abundant wildlife here: turtles (some surprisingly large), wood ducks and other species of ducks, great blue herons, snowy and common egrets, kingfishers, cormorants, and occasional bald eagles. The lake is managed as a trophy bass lake, so all smaller bass must be returned to the water. The result of this is the potential for some very large bass, along with pickerel and nice-sized bluegills. Recently, I have noticed bass going after dragonflies and damselflies on the surface in weedy areas near the shoreline, and I have been

A Mauch Chunk bass.

experimenting with tying flies to imitate these insects. I am looking forward to catching a really nice largemouth bass on a dry fly!

FAIRVIEW LAKE, PENNSYLVANIA

It is a tradition in our family to celebrate Columbus Day with a getaway get-together with our close friends Tom and Margaret. In our younger years, before children, these were always camping trips along the Big Flatbrook, a trout stream in northern New Jersey, or in a state park in Connecticut where Kathy and I lived. Later, these trips centered around cabins for rent in the Poconos in Pennsylvania. Our tradition was interrupted when Kathy and I moved to Montana for two years, prior to moving back

Fairview Lake on an autumn morning.

east to the Poconos. Since then, our tradition has resumed with an annual meeting in a cottage along the shore of Fairview Lake, near Hawley, Pennsylvania, and Lake Wallenpaupack.

Although we typically spin fish during these stays at the cabin, with mixed success, I used the backpack fly-fishing strategy on one special occasion. A few years ago, I realized that I had owned my first fly rod for thirty years, so I decided it was time to celebrate it and my original spinning rod. I brought both to the cabin, along with my backpack and a birthday card to recognize their thirty years of fun times. We had had a particularly slow and unsuccessful fishing trip over the first day and a half of our stay. On that second evening Tom and I were fishing from the dock by the cabin, he with spinning gear and I with Trusty and a Chief Needabeh, a red and yellow attractor streamer pattern that I had tied for the occasion but never previously used. I had cast several times without success when I noticed a nice bass clearly visible near the dock. It was truly a gift in honor of the occasion. I cast over the bass and stripped the streamer past his head. He followed and lunged twice, each time missing the mark, before he caught up to the streamer and I caught him—a beautiful 10.75-inch bass. We returned again this year and, once again, my original fly rod was successful in catching a smallmouth bass and several sunfish, all on #16 Hairwing Henryville Specials. Tom brought his fly rod also, and he caught several bigger sunfish on the same pattern, all from the dock on a warm and sunny October afternoon.

WHITE CITY LAKE, NEW JERSEY

As Tom mentioned in the foreword, my first experiences with fly fishing took place on White City Lake in Trenton, New Jersey. This is truly my "point of origin" in terms of fly fishing, and I have never forgotten the earthy smells and the sounds of a pond in spring time: the calls of red-winged blackbirds, the popping sounds of bluegills hitting the top of the water, the occasional splash of a larger fish out near the middle, and the soundless swooping of bats over the water at dusk. We had to wade out into the lake by balancing on the roots of lily pads, which was a process of feeling your way with your feet. We looked for likely areas where patches of open water lay among the dense lily pads. From our vantage point, these looked like bays of water as seen from an aircraft flying over swamplands, and we took to referring to specific open areas by names, such as "calico bay." It was on this lake that I learned the true essence of fly fishing: tying on a fly that seems likely to work, locating a spot of open water, aiming, and then casting. If the fly hit the mark, then it was a matter of waiting for a fish to strike. I learned that this sport required my full concentration and now, so many years later, it is still one of the best ways to drive other cares and concerns from my mind, at least during the time that I am fishing. Our first successful experience on White City Lake still serves as Tom's and my yardstick for a truly memorable and fun fly-fishing experience.

FARM POND IN NORTHERN NEW JERSEY

Tom's wife Margaret grew up on a farm in rural northern New Jersey. A stream-fed pond is a central feature of the farm, and Tom has spent decades fishing it for the largemouth bass that live there, some of them enormous. Pickerel also live there, but Tom is after bass. I fished with him there on the early morning of his wedding day, hours before he and Margaret were married by the side of the pond. I have heard his stories of fishing there for years.

Several years ago, Tom called to tell me that they were up at the farm and that we should come over. We arrived early in the morning, and Tom and I went out in the old rowboat. I was deep in my interest in tying and fishing bass flies, so I brought my 8-weight and left my

The farm pond at dawn.

spinning gear at home. This is Tom's home water and, as the morning progressed, Tom caught bass after bass, each seeming to be bigger than the one before it. I had caught nothing and started to suspect that I would go home empty-handed. Finally, at Tom's suggestion, I looked in my small box of bass flies and selected a purple rabbit-strip diver, which is a floating fly that resembles a water snake. I had tied it months before and saw little reason to try it, but I did nonetheless. I cast it underneath a big overhanging branch of the tree that grew by the shore, and then slowly retrieved the fly across the surface. The 13-inch largemouth bass that engulfed the fly was the first that I ever caught on a fly rod and, although much smaller than those that Tom caught, was an inspiration to keep trying and experimenting.

We returned to the pond recently and, again, Tom guided me to the best spots. I had a small assortment of flies and my 8-weight fly rod, and we cast from the family's rowboat. I was fortunate to catch several personal bests (for bluegill, common sunfish, pickerel, and yellow perch), all on the same day—an incredible day of fly fishing on a unique and beautiful pond.

JUROVATY'S POND, CONNECTICUT

I fished this pond extensively with both Tom and my friend Ernie when I lived in Connecticut. Typically, we would fish for bass with spinning rods and rubber worms from my canoe, *Tiger Lily*. After extensive exploration of the pond on multiple occasions, it became clear that the most productive area was a long line of thick weeds that lined the left-hand side of the lake. Although the majority of our fishing here was with spinning rods, I began to bring a fly rod and a small box of bass and panfish flies. I was most successful in catching large bluegills on the surface using small Gaines cork poppers. On one occasion, I also caught a nice 14-inch pickerel on one of the first frog deer hair bugs that I had ever tied. At the time that I fished this pond, I still associated fly fishing with trout, and my interest in and experience with bass fly fishing was just beginning. In hindsight, I wish that I had spent more time fishing here with a fly rod. When we moved out west to Montana, I missed my times on Jurovaty's Pond and the opportunities for warmwater fly fishing, despite the tremendous trout fishing in Montana.

MANSFIELD HOLLOW LAKE, CONNECTICUT

I fished here from the shore when we first moved to Connecticut. As with many lakes that hold warmwater fish, Mansfield Hollow Lake offered a mixed bag of fish, including bass, pickerel, and sunfish. I fished there on a number of occasions, sometimes hiking through the woods behind our apartment to get to the lake, and typically I would catch bluegills and common sunfish on dry flies. I was just starting to become a competent enough fly-tier to be able to use my own flies, and it felt like a real achievement to fool a fish on something that I had created. It was here where I caught my first ever pickerel, 13 inches long, on a Montana stonefly nymph that I had tied. On another trip, I taught a visiting friend, who had never fly fished in his life, to catch bluegills on dry flies.

LITTLE PINE CREEK, PENNSYLVANIA

Little Pine State Park in central Pennsylvania is a small park and campground centered around Little Pine Creek. This is a notable trout stream that is a tributary of the larger Pine Creek, one of the major trout streams of Pennsylvania. Below Little Pine Lake (an impoundment of Little Pine Creek), where the campground is located, Little Pine Creek continues on its southerly course toward its confluence with Pine Creek. When we first moved to Pennsylvania, we camped there for our summer vacation when our sons were quite young. Because Little Pine Creek was an easy walk from the tent site, I could go down to take a few casts without a major commitment of time away from my family. As I described earlier in my discussion of smallmouth bass, this is where I had a great time casting a Black Ghost streamer into the seam between the faster water on the far side of the creek and the slower water on my side. This is another example of the usefulness of backpack fly fishing, because I had no preconceived notions about the stream when I first encountered it. It was described as a productive and popular trout stream, but my prospecting with a streamer in the warm August weather resulted in success with hard fighting stream smallmouth bass, one of the most enjoyable fish of all to catch.

POHOPOCO CREEK, PENNSYLVANIA

I consider Pohopoco Creek, also known locally as the Big Creek, to be my first "home water" in the Poconos. I caught my first Pennsylvania trout here and have fished it on many occasions. It flows southwesterly, entering Beltzville Lake, a man-made lake created by an Army Corps of Engineers dam, below which the stream continues as a tailwater fishery before winding its way to its confluence with the Lehigh River. Above the lake, it harbors wild trout but, as it slows near the top of the lake, it holds warmwater fish. I have fished this slow area with small cork poppers for bass and sunfish. I recall one warm summer evening at dusk when I fished from the banks underneath an overpassing road. The slow water swirled gently around the bridge pilings while a great horned owl called from somewhere in the deep woods and a little green heron flew along the stream. It was mesmerizing to watch the white cork popper drift slowly with the current while I gave it occasional twitches with small pulls on the fly line. And it offered the familiar, fun game of waiting for the bluegills that attacked the surface popper, three of which I caught that evening.

BELLEVILLE POND, RHODE ISLAND

I fished this small pond near my parents' home from shore using spinning gear, from a canoe, and later from shore with my fly rod. On one memorable occasion, many years ago, I waded into the water where a small stream entered the pond. I had been experimenting with fly tying for the first time, and I created a dry fly with red and yellow buck-

A sunfish in its element.

tail wings and tail and a black fur-dubbed body. Naturally, I called it the Belleville Special. It was neither a thing of beauty nor particularly well tied, but it worked. I cast the fly in the direction of the water entering the pond and let it drift along the natural feeding lane. This resulted in several terrific, hard fighting bluegills, including a 9-inch beauty that stood as a personal best until just recently. This experience helped me to learn that, when water is entering a lake via a stream or brook, this is often the best place to approach and then cast a fly. In this case, there was no animation on my part, as the stream's current carried the fly to where the bluegills and other fish were waiting for food.

TURNER'S LAKE, NEW JERSEY

Turner's lake is in a private residential area in northern New Jersey. I was able to fish it during a Fourth of

July gathering of my wife's family several years ago. The party was an all-day event and I knew that I would have an opportunity to take a few casts, so I had brought my 8-weight rod and a box of bass poppers in my backpack. When my son Brendan and I became restless just sitting and conversing with family members, we took a walk down by the lake and fished a small cove. It was quite weedy here, with a large fallen branch that stuck out into the water. I tied on an orange and white spun deer hair bass bug that I had tied, took a few casts to a likely area by the fallen branch, and was rewarded with a foot-long largemouth bass. I then switched to a Gaines cork popper and caught four nice bluegills in the 7- to 8-inch range. I returned my equipment to the backpack and put it back into my car before Bren and I returned to the party. We were gone less than half an hour, and I don't think anyone had missed us.

HIDDEN LAKE, PENNSYLVANIA

When I was recovering from my hip replacement operation in 2011, Kathy and I tried a series of short excursions to area parks to get me out of the house and moving more regularly. At that point in my recovery, I was still actively engaged in physical therapy and had to use a cane for any walking. These trips were instrumental in motivating me to continue to improve my mobility, since I missed fishing and outdoor activities. Hidden Lake, within the Delaware Water Gap National Recreation Area, was only the second lake that I tried to fish less than two months after my operation. We parked by a picnic and fishing area on a July morning and walked slowly down to the edge of the lake. Although a trail circumnavigates the lake, my limited mobility restricted me to the picnic table grove by the parking lot. My approach was slow and entailed me getting as close to the edge of the water as I could with my limited mobility and my cane. I selected a McGinty wet fly (just because I like it) and cast straight out toward some vegetation and lily pads close to shore. Because of the shrubbery along the shoreline, I had to rely on short roll casts, and my fly did not get too far out from shore, but I was rewarded with three small but beautiful bluegills. A week later, we fished Tobyhanna Lake on the Pocono Plateau in the same manner, and again I caught small bluegills near the shore of that lake. In my fish journal, I came to call this series of trips my "bluegill summer," and I am absolutely convinced that these fishing trips were highly instrumental in my recovery from major surgery.

Coastal Saltwater Fishing

I have had far less experience with coastal saltwater fishing than I have with fresh waters. However, the steps of the backpack fly-fishing approach lend themselves equally well to these environments and fish. If I lived along the coast near the ocean, I would undoubtedly keep a heavier fly rod, say an 8-weight, and a small box of Epoxy Minnows and Clouser Deep Minnows ready for wading the shoreline in search of fish. These fish, including striped bass and bluefish, are almost always in search of minnows

Saltwater estuaries can be productive areas to fish.

and other smaller fish, so saltwater streamers are the go-to flies.

WICKFORD HARBOR, RHODE ISLAND

It is somewhat embarrassing to admit that, although my family owned a home on Wickford Harbor off Narragansett Bay, I did not pay any attention to the potential for fly-fishing offered by the water right outside their yard. In fact, it took the opening of a fly-fishing shop right in town to set the lightbulb off: there are fish in the bay and they can be caught with a fly rod. One summer when my family and I were visiting my mother, I had brought my

8-weight rod to fish Belleville Pond for largemouth bass, and a walk up to the aforementioned fly shop turned my attention toward the bay. I bought two or three Clouser Deep Minnows in chartreuse and white and enlisted my young sons to join in the harbor in front of my mom's home in our dinghy, *Tippy*. We rowed slowly among the moored sailing yachts while trolling the deep minnow. No casting was involved, and I let my sons take turns holding the fly rod. When the first hit and hookup came, it was a shock to me because I was not used to the size and power of saltwater fish. That first fish, a smallish striped bass of about 25 inches, dove deep, wrapped the leader around a mooring buoy chain, and then broke off the heavy 16-pound test leader. From there, we learned quickly that high tides brought the fish into the cove and, over the next several days, we caught thirty striped bass that we measured and released, all between 14 and 25 inches long. For the first time, I had to actually use the drag on a fly reel to slow these powerful fish. I later learned that real saltwater fishers considered these fish to be small stuff and called them "schoolies," not to be confused with the enormous striped bass and bluefish that they pursued. During that summer, and the four after it prior to my mom's death in 2003, we fished from *Tippy* or I wet-waded and fished from shore. Sometimes, we caught stripers and at other times small bluefish.

Among the lessons that I learned over those summers was the importance of looking for signs of fish from other wildlife: for example, fleeing minnows jumping in schools clear of the water indicated pursuing striped bass or bluefish. Likewise, birds congregating in a specific area indicated fish were nearby. I later used these signs to locate fish in other places as well, as I did once on the Pohopoco Creek by using diving kingfishers to guide me to trout in a riffled area of the stream. Like all living things in a natural environment, fish are connected to other forms of life, weather patterns, and seasonal variations, and knowledge of these other forces only helps open our eyes to what is happening below the surface where we cannot see.

Summary

The purpose of this chapter is to give you a flavor of the range of situations in which the ASCAL steps of the backpack fly-fishing approach may be used. The events that I have described took place over many years and under a wide variety of circumstances in my life. However, there were many commonalities to them. First, during each of these situations I was using a fly rod and a small box—or even handful—of flies. Very little other equipment was necessary. Second, many of the situations that I have described entailed a process of prospecting and discovery, as I did not know in advance what type of fish I might encounter or where they might be. This leads to another common element, which is the need to pay attention to clues in the natural environment, whether they are birds, other fish, or features of a stream or pond that might lead to fish. And, finally, as I look back on these events, I am struck once again by the fact that *all* of the fish that I caught (or lost) were fascinating and beautiful creatures.

Chapter Six

Oh, and by the Way . . .
Additional Considerations and Concerns

In this chapter, we will discuss additional issues, concerns, and considerations that we should take into account when getting ready to go backpack fly fishing. Specifically, we will cover the following:

- Strategies for identifying when and where to go backpack fly fishing
- Fly selections that might work best for you, including my recommended "basic" fly selection, as well as some more specialty variations
- The benefits of tying your own flies, including a few that my family or I have developed or adapted from existing flies
- Important safety considerations
- The importance and fun of maintaining and referring to a fishing journal
- The use of wildlife photography to enhance your experiences

- Steps to take to minimize your negative impact on the environment and future fishing opportunities
- Some comments on using backpack fishing principles for spin fishing
- Activities for the off-season that enhance your backpack fly-fishing experiences

When and Where to Backpack Fly Fish

FINDING PLACES TO BACKPACK FLY FISH

People who fish are constantly looking for promising places to try, and the same is true for backpack flyfishers. One of the clear advantages of backpack fly fishing is that, as long as you have your backpack with you, you will be ready to fish any time that you happen upon a nice place. I have found that some of the best ways to find places to fly fish are to use maps, guides for state or national parks, or local guides to places to hike, fish, camp, or watch birds or other wildlife. In addition, prospecting or exploring possible encouraging spots to try has yielded a surprising number of good fishing experiences for me.

Maps are one of the first resources to consult in looking for places to backpack fly fish. Although a national atlas will provide you with fair maps of each state and province, at some point it is preferable to locate a full-sized, more detailed map of the area that you are investigating. Detailed atlases of each state, published by DeLorme Mapping Company, allow a close investigation of local roads and streams. Also, I suggest that you try your local town

Where to start looking for places to fish.

hall or township office to obtain a more detailed map of your town, township, or county. These are typically free and give you much more detail than a state map can. It may also be worth finding a topographical map of your local area; these are typically available at stores dedicated to serious outdoor sports such as camping, climbing, kayaking, or cycling. I find that, often, I need to consult more than one map of an area to get a better idea about the roads that approach bodies of water and where those waters might be accessed. I love maps and often enjoy spending quite a bit of time studying both familiar and unfamiliar areas to get a better idea of the lay of the land before heading out.

In addition to general maps, guides to state and national parks can be extremely helpful in locating possible places to hike in and fish. We are very fortunate in our area in the Poconos of eastern Pennsylvania to have the Delaware Water Gap National Recreation area and several excellent state parks within an hour's drive from home. Each of these parks offers more than one possible place to fish, and each provides a free guide that describes the unique features of the park, wildlife that live there, and fish that inhabit the waters. Also, these guides provide maps of the parks that show hiking trails and campground areas. Such maps are invaluable because they provide information about how to access streams and ponds from different points on hiking trails. This is particularly useful information, as you can find great places to fish that are not as frequently accessed by other people. If you visit a state or national park, make sure to put a copy of their guide in your backpack and keep it there for future visits. We have recently started a file of these guides that we have accumulated over the years for future reference.

A third resource for locating places to backpack fly fish are guidebooks on fishing, hiking, camping, and bird and wildlife identification within your state or region. Although books specifically focused on places to fish within your state or area may be useful, don't overlook those books that focus on other activities. In particular, I have found that guides to the best places to hike usually mention streams or ponds that may be encountered on each hike. The same is true of guides to places to camp or to locate, observe, and photograph birds and wildlife. Because much of my fishing happens when I am hiking, camping, or bird-watching, these guides are great for finding areas to visit, and I almost always have my backpack with me, just in case.

In addition to all of the above resources, I cannot overestimate the importance of just prospecting and keeping track of places as you hike, camp, or travel. I am always on the lookout for potential new places for future trips. For example, for the past nineteen years, we have meant to visit the western part of Pennsylvania, specifically an area where Rocky Mountain elk were reintroduced into our state. These magnificent animals were eradicated in the mid-1800s, but were reintroduced to the Elk County area in western Pennsylvania during the early to mid-twentieth century. We finally made the trip recently and were rewarded by seeing

A western Pennsylvania elk.

numerous bull and cow elk, and by finally hearing our first elk bugle. While in the area, I was able to start to familiarize myself with some of the local trout streams that I had read about in my books about trout fishing in Pennsylvania. Also, a visit to a county visitor center provided information on nearby Allegheny National Forest, a vast wild area just west of the Elk County area. This area has much potential for future hiking, camping, and fishing expeditions, and we are already starting to make some tentative plans for another visit there sometime in the future.

WHEN TO GO BACKPACK FLY FISHING

In general, any time you encounter some likely looking water, and have your backpack with your rod and reel and a few flies with you, is a good time to try fishing. Having said that, my fishing experiences using my backpack fall into the categories of those that were planned in advance and those that were not.

If I know that we are driving or hiking to a lake or stream that I have fished before or that, having consulted maps and guides, I know has promise for good fishing, I will bring my backpack with me with the intention of fishing. We may also be hiking, camping, or having a picnic lunch, but at some point I know that I will take a few casts, and I may well even know where the best spots to try will be.

On other occasions, however, I really have no intention of fishing, or it certainly is not a main priority for our outing. I have learned from many experiences during which I *did not* bring my backpack that it is easy to miss opportunities in some of the most promising and prettiest looking places. So, if at all in doubt, I bring the backpack. I do so enough that I would estimate that I do not even open my backpack to take out fishing equipment on about half of the trips on which I bring it.

I credit my father for this idea of always having a fishing rod handy. Although he did not fish, he knew that I enjoyed it and supported me through occasional gifts related to fishing, such as my first fly tying kit, first real fly box, books on fly tying and fishing, and a pack spin-cast rod that packs into an incredibly small box. Although I gravitate to fly fishing, this first pack rod, and my dad's advice to leave it in my car "just in case," really helped to shape my interest in backpack fishing.

BACKPACK FLY FISHING FROM A CANOE OR BOAT

In some ways, fishing from a canoe or boat is a very different experience than hiking in with a backpack. However, there are times when Kathy and I go out in the canoe to one of our favorite local lakes, and I bring my pack, rod, and a box of flies to try while she photographs or identifies birds and other wildlife. On these trips, I may or may not plan in advance to fish. I can recall one trip a couple of years ago during which I brought my backpack but the lake was too deep to lend itself to fly fishing, although I did fish during a later hike on a trail around it. On other occasions, I will be familiar with a lake and know that it holds nice fish and I would be there specifically to fish for them. The pack that I bring in the canoe is actually smaller than my backpack and is designed to hold a few flies, along with sunscreen, needle-nosed pliers, and so forth. These situations do fit the basic premise of the backpack fly-fishing approach: a single backpack with a fly rod and reel and one box of flies.

Fly Selections

THE BASIC FLY COLLECTION

In chapter 4 we briefly discussed what I consider to be the basic fly box collection for a single backpack fly-fishing box. These include dry flies, wet flies, nymphs, streamers, and bass poppers. Table 6.1 shows my preferences for the flies in which I have most confidence and that I use most frequently. Most of these are ones that I use because (a)

TABLE 6.1	
My Basic Fly Collection	
Type of Fly	**My Favorite Choices**
Dry Flies	Henryville Special (Hairwing Henryville)
	Light Cahill
	Adams
Wet Flies	Professor
	Royal Coachman
	Iron Blue Dun
	Partridge and Orange
Streamers	Black Ghost and Black Ghost Marabou
	Mickey Finn
	Grey Ghost
	Chief Needabeh
	Green Glitterer
	Blue Sunrise
Nymphs	Pheasant Tail Nymph
	Gold Ribbed Hare's Ear Nymph
	Montana Stonefly Nymph
Bass Poppers	Small Gaines Poppers in sunfish and small bass sizes
	Deerhair bass bugs, #6

I can tie them myself, and (b) they have worked, consistently, in a variety of situations with a variety of fish.

At this point, if you haven't done so already, you can develop your own basic fly collection and adapt it to the area in which you live or fish most frequently. If you have no fly-fishing experience whatsoever, then you might want to start with the one I have provided here. You will undoubtedly find some, if not all, of these flies useful to you as you gain experience. However, also feel free to ask people in sporting goods or fly-fishing shops for good all-around flies that will work. Remember that you are not asking for a specific fly that matches a short-lived insect hatch, but for tried-and-true flies that work day in and day out. If you have some fly-fishing experience, then start to build your basic fly collection by choosing those flies that have worked for you most consistently or that you find yourself reaching for when you first open your fly boxes.

By the way, if you are currently an experienced fly-fisher with a vest full of fly boxes and you want to start backpack fly fishing, I *strongly* discourage you from simply transferring all of your fly boxes from your vest to a backpack. This will accomplish nothing, and you may as well keep them in your vest. Instead, go ahead and buy the best all-around single box that you think will hold your basic collection of flies and start filling it. If you tie your own flies, this will give you yet another reason to tie some more of your favorites.

REGIONAL VARIATIONS

Although the vast majority of your backpack fly fishing can and should be completed with your basic fly collection, sometimes you will have opportunities to fish for specific types of fish that call for more specialized fly collections. On those occasions, it is okay to alter your basic collection or even bring one small, extra box with a few specialized flies in it.

For example, if I know that I am going to hike into a lake that has nice largemouth bass in it, possibly lingering near some lily pads by the shore, I might well bring a few extra deer hair bass bugs to use, because they work and they are fun to use to catch bass on the surface of the water. Incidentally, I also will probably bring a heavier fly rod, such as my 8- or 9-weight, and heavier leaders, such as 0x or 1x. I will still have my basic collection with me, but I will carry these extra flies because I know that I am likely to have a chance to catch a larger largemouth bass if I use a few larger bass bugs.

Our trips to Cape Breton Highlands National Park in Nova Scotia, described previously, provide another example of regional variations on the basic fly collection. When I traveled there most recently, I knew that I would be fishing for brook (speckled) trout with wet flies. Although I carried my basic collection in my backpack, I also brought a single box of just wet flies and a few streamers, because I knew that I would not use any other types of flies, so this simplified things for me. On that same trip, I knew that I would hike into the Cheticamp River and take a few casts in the wild hopes of catching an Atlantic salmon. (Alas, not this time . . .) So, my fly box also included my small collection of salmon flies, with a couple of extra Mickey Finns tied onto traditional black salmon streamer hooks with their turned-up eyes.

The Benefits of Tying Your Own Flies

As I stated in the first chapter, one of the main reasons that I am drawn to fly fishing is that I have the opportunity to catch fish with something that I created. From the moment

I tried my first fly, before I even knew how to wind on tying thread with a bobbin, I was intrigued by the idea of creating something out of bits of fur, feathers, and other materials that would look alive. Catching my first bluegills and calico bass on my own flies felt like a tremendous achievement, and I felt the same when I caught my first trout on a Montana Stonefly nymph that I had tied. Later, I experienced similar satisfaction in catching a largemouth bass on a spun deer hair bass bug that I had tied. Over the past thirty-odd years, I have taken a few fly tying lessons and collected a fair number of books on fly tying. These have opened the doors to a fun, engaging, and relaxing hobby that is connected to but distinct from fishing. Fly tying has sustained me through many a late fall, deep winter, and early spring morning when it was impossible to get out to fish. I have tied more flies than I will ever use, and I keep tying more because, like most hobbies, most of the fun is in trying to improve my skills. And I still much prefer to catch a fish on a fly that I have tied.

There are numerous fly tying guides for beginning, intermediate, and advanced fly-tiers, and my intent here is not to duplicate that material. (See the section on further reading for a couple of my favorite fly tying books.) However, I have adapted flies that I use quite a bit, and both of my sons created unique streamer patterns that have worked for me; thus, I have included descriptions of these flies below.

As stated in chapter 4, I rely heavily on caddis fly patterns for dry fly fishing, and the Henryville Special is the caddis imitation that I like best. I liked this pattern for years before I moved to Pennsylvania, when I discovered that Henryville is actually a town near mine. I also learned that the fly had, in fact, been invented for the Brodhead Creek here in the Poconos, one of the earliest centers of American fly fishing. The only change to the fly that I have included is to use different wing material. The completed fly, which I call the Hairwing Henryville, is made of the following:

- dry fly hook, #14 to #20
- green or orange floss body
- grizzly hackle tied in at the bend and wound forward
- white synthetic hair fibers for the wing
- dark brown hackle in front of the wing

The "Hairwing" Henryville Special.

This fly is, above all others, the one that I would turn to if I had to have only one.

Another fly that is fun to adapt is a spun deer hair bass popper. You can tie these in any color combination, but I have enjoyed combining orange, red, and black deer hair with saddle hackle and Krystal Flash tails (or legs). I add weed guards made of heavier monofilament line because I fish around lily pads for largemouth bass. Try any color combination. They are extremely messy to tie, but it is great fun to "sculpt" a bass bug out of a puffball of spun deer hair.

My sons Brendan and Zach both tried fly tying for a while in their youth—long enough to create their own unique streamer patterns. Neither is particularly based on nature; rather, they reflect the innate creativity of young kids. I have tried them both (specifically, I have used them to catch wild brook trout in New Brunswick) and, in fact, they can both catch fish. It is a new level of fun to catch a fish on flies that you tied and that your children invented. Below is what they look like and the materials needed to tie them:

Green Glitterer (Brendan Steere)

- streamer hook, #12 to #14
- body of flat silver Mylar with round silver ribbing
- three or four strands of peacock herl tied in as an underwing and extending from the head to just beyond the bend of the hook
- a bunch of green Flashabou (approximately fifteen to eighteen strands) as a wing

The Green Glitterer.

- (Note: Brendan also created the same fly using gold Flashabou, which he called the Gold Glitterer.)

Blue Sunrise (Zach Steere)
- streamer hook, #12 to #14
- tail of several fibers of deep blue saddle hackle
- body of orange floss with a gold rib
- wing of two dark blue saddle hackles
- beard or collar of orange hackle

These flies are not the height of originality, but they reflect an important point: fly tying, like fly fishing itself, should be a process of discovery and adaptation. It is fun to try to adapt existing flies to make them work better or easier to tie, and it is also fun to create new ones. Unless you are aiming to become a master fly-tier, you do not

The Blue Sunrise.

have to be a slave to existing patterns tied only with traditional materials. I love traditional flies, but I also love adapting them or even inventing new ones.

Important Safety Considerations

Like any outdoor sport, backpack fly fishing can present some safety hazards, and it is important to be prepared for them by anticipating and preventing them. The main safety hazards are those due to falls while hiking, casting accidents, exposure to sun, and exposure to poisonous plants.

Any time I am hiking, particularly on uneven, rocky, or leaf-covered ground, falls are a potential hazard. I became particularly aware of these hazards after recovering from hip replacement surgery. I have also found that what I could do in my twenties is not necessarily what I am capable of in my sixties. Eyesight, balance, and strength change over time. As a result, I make a point of being far more careful while walking and hiking. If the ground is rocky or uneven, I now carry a hiking staff for additional stability and support. Also, if I want to admire the scenery or try to spot a bird that I have heard calling, I stop walking first and then look, because, if I don't, I am likely to trip and fall.

Fly fishing has the inherent danger that a back cast or forward cast can end up putting a hook into you. I found this out the hard way almost thirty years ago while fishing a local lake. I was in the process of casting when I heard a loud splash to my immediate left. Instinctively, I turned toward the sound while my back cast was in progress. Big mistake! The result was that my fly, a particularly gaudy Yellow Sally, ended up embedded into the very tip of my nose. Fortunately, I always de-barb my hooks, so the hook came out easily without a trip to the emergency room. Although the incident is funny in hindsight (and my wife thought it was *very* funny at the time), I was inches away from potential eye damage. The obvious moral of the story is not to turn, walk, or change directions while casting. Also, be particularly careful whenever the wind starts to blow. It is important to be in control of your cast and to know where the fly is at all times.

Because sun is a hazard any time we are exposed to it, I always carry sunscreen and use it, unless it is early or late in the day. It is always helpful to have it in my pack, because I can share it with others who may have forgotten it.

If you are unsure if a plant is poisonous, such as poison ivy, it is best to avoid it while hiking. Try to learn to identify the poisonous plants in your area and how they look during different seasons.

In general, fishing and hiking with someone else is preferable because you have someone there to help in case of an accident or injury. However, that is not always possible, so extra care should be taken while you are hiking or fishing alone to prevent problems from happening.

The Importance and Fun of Using and Maintaining a Fishing Journal

Starting with the very first fish that I caught as a young adult, I have always kept records of my catches. Sometimes my records are pretty sketchy ("five little sunfish"), but over the years I have tried to be more consistent in recording how many fish I have caught, what I caught them on, and their length.

I have found that there are many benefits to maintaining a fishing journal. First, it is a fun way to reward myself for a successful day of fishing. I like to write down what I caught as soon as I get home, along with notes on the weather, other wildlife, water temperature, and so forth. I also use ink stamps to note personal best catches. Although a somewhat silly practice, it reminds me of the captains' logs of old whaling ships, where each whale caught was recorded in a primitive picture in the log. A second reason for maintaining a fishing journal is that, in doing so, you create your own guide to the best times and places to go fishing in the future. On many occasions, my friend Tom has joked about my fishing journals and the accuracy of my fish measurements, but he also turns to me when he wants to remember when we went on a particular fishing trip and what we used. A third reason is that it is fun in the dead of winter to read back through past entries, because they constitute a personal history of the good times of fishing with important people in my life. If I did not maintain my fishing journal, there is no way that I would remember the length in inches of the largest of each of the types of fish that I have caught, where I caught them, or what I used to catch them. Fortunately, I don't have to search my memory, because it is all in my fishing journals.

The Benefit of Wildlife Photography

As the development of small, high-resolution digital cameras has advanced, I have found that it is easier to record

A bald eagle at Mauch Chunk Lake.

fishing trips visually. Typically, if I am alone, I carry a small point-and-shoot digital camera in my backpack. Sometimes I will use it to photograph the lake or river that I am fishing, just because the scenery is beautiful and the fishing slow. I have also found that this type of camera is of such quality that I can hold a fish in my left hand and take a quality photograph of it with my right hand (assuming that the fish cooperates and holds still long enough). Increasingly, I have found that the addition of photography to the backpack fly-fishing experience adds a lot to my enjoyment.

When Kathy and I go together, she always carries her camera and is often focused more on taking pictures and locating and identifying birds. Likewise, if my son Zach is with us, he is frequently snapping photos. As attested to by the photographs in this book, their work has helped to document some beautiful fish and wildlife and the places in which they live.

Minimizing Your Impact on the Environment

Whenever we are engaging in sports outdoors, it is important to live by the rule to leave a place in as good or better condition as you found it. Trash and litter should always be thrown away or packed out, particularly leader material that can hurt ducks and other wildlife. If necessary, you can carry a small bag in your backpack in which to put leader material and other trash.

Catch and release fishing makes sense and should be practiced whenever possible. It is important to use barbless hooks and release fish as quickly and carefully as possible.

A Note on Backpack Spin Fishing

In this book, I have chosen to focus on fly fishing, primarily because I enjoy it and the challenges that fly fishing and fly tying present. However, the same principles that we have covered in this book also apply to spin fishing. The steps of the ASCAL method—approach, select a lure, cast, animate, and land—apply easily to the use of spinning gear and lures. So, if you enjoy spin fishing, then by all means use the backpack fishing approach. In fact, as mentioned previously, my father's gift of a Daiwa Minicast rod and reel was important in the development of my interest in backpack fishing, and I sometimes still use that rod and reel.

If you do decide to pack a spinning rod, you will have to develop your optimal collection of lures that might work in the widest range of situations. If you include rubber worms or similar lures, make sure to use a "wormproof" box, that is, one that will not melt upon contact with the chemicals in rubber worms. The lures that come to mind for me would include:

- small marabou jigs in a variety of colors
- small and medium spinners or spoons
- a few rubber worms in dark colors
- a couple of hooks and small sinkers for possible bait fishing

One of the reasons that I gravitate toward fly fishing is that I don't like to use treble hooks. My main objection to them is that they are inherently more dangerous to both fish and me. Lures with double sets of treble hooks are even more of a hazard. Therefore, I strongly suggest that you look for lures that have single hooks instead of treble hooks. Although I have not taken the time to try this myself to see how it works, I imagine that treble hooks on lures could be removed and replaced with single hooks, although this may affect the action of the lures.

During the Off-Season

As I write this paragraph, it is in the middle of the off-season here in the Poconos. It is deep winter and, despite a temporary thaw, there is snow on the ground and more on the way, along with frigid temperatures. Although some hardy souls may attempt ice fishing this time of year, for me it is not a time for fishing.

But it is a time for many other activities that will lead to more fun with backpack fly fishing once the spring rolls around. In some ways, I love the off-season because it opens up opportunities to plan, explore, prospect, and dream. As you have probably figured out if you have read this far, my philosophy of fly fishing is to tie it into as many other activities as possible. Backpack fly fishing is by its nature a generalist activity that incorporates hiking, identification of trees, shrubs, and wildflowers; bird-watching and observation of animals; identification of animal tracks; canoeing; camping; fly tying; and photography. Many, if not most of these, can be done during the off-season, even if you aren't up for fishing with frozen hands. Below are some of the many things that you can do when it is not quite time to fish.

HIKING/SNOWSHOEING

Even when it is far too cold to fish, it is fun and great exercise to hike or snowshoe. I discovered snowshoeing a few years ago and I have found that, for me, it is preferable to other winter sports such as cross-country skiing or skating. Snowshoeing and hiking are wonderful ways to get out and explore places to fish next year. For example, there is a local park about half an hour from our house with

A stream in deep winter, and the promise for spring fishing.

a beautiful hike along a stream. I have yet to fish it, but just seeing it, even in the dead of winter, gets me thinking about the possibilities.

An additional benefit of hiking or snow shoeing through the snow is that it is easier to spot and to try to identify animal tracks in the snow. I am a novice at this, but I enjoy spotting rabbit, deer, and even different bird tracks in the snow. Again, these just give you clues to what types of wildlife live in that environment during the harsh winter.

BIRD-WATCHING

As I have discussed throughout this book, locating and identifying birds is a terrific hobby in and of itself, and it can be done all year. It is fun to keep a life list in order to keep track of all of the birds that you have seen and where you have seen them. Increasingly, we have added the challenge of photographing birds that we have spotted. Also, as mentioned previously, observations of bird behavior, particularly those that eat fish, such as herons, egrets, kingfishers, bald eagles, and osprey, can often clue us in to best places and times to fish in local bodies of water.

STUDYING MAPS AND FIELD GUIDES

I love maps and can spend a lot of time studying them. As I mentioned earlier in this chapter, this is one of the best ways to start to narrow down places for future fishing trips, and you can review maps and field guides even in the deepest winter.

GETTING EQUIPMENT READY

Finally, it is worth spending time during the off-season to organize and prepare your equipment for the following spring. I completely empty my backpack, throw out any scraps of old leaders, empty leader packets and other trash, and check the condition of the rods and fly lines. Because cold weather can really hurt a fly line, I make sure to bring all of my fly lines and leaders in from the garage to a warmer area during the colder months. Winter is also an ideal time to check and restock your fly box and, if you are running low on a particularly reliable fly, it is a great time to spend a few hours tying flies for spring.

Summary

This chapter has touched on a number of different topics related to having fun while backpack fly fishing.

First, we discussed a number of ways to identify promising places to fly fish and when to do so. Learning about areas closer to or farther from home almost inevitably leads to discovery of additional places to try. Using maps, park brochures, and field guides can be extremely useful and can happen any time of year.

If you like the idea of tying your own flies but have not ever tried it, I suggest picking up an introductory guide to fly patterns and a beginner's fly tying kit. From there it is simply a matter of practice and experience. I have included a couple of excellent fly tying guides in the section of for further reading.

Whether you tie your own flies of not, you will need to develop your own personal collection of go-to flies in which you have confidence and that cover the widest range of situations. This process of selection is never ending and is one of the most fun aspects of the backpack fly-fishing process.

Safety is a must, and the simple strategies that I discussed here can help prevent injuries from occurring.

Finally, the off-season is a great time to engage in a range of activities that do not involve fly-fishing equipment but that will enhance your knowledge and appreciation of the outdoors and wildlife and that will inspire you to try again next spring.

Afterword

A Different Way of Thinking

As I stated at the outset of this book, backpack fly fishing is not the only way to enjoy fishing, but it is a legitimate and important alternative. Our world is increasingly complex, with more technology, more passwords to remember, and more tasks in our everyday lives. Sometimes a step back to simplicity is needed, and this approach fulfills that need.

As we look back at all that we have covered in this book, let's summarize the key points to remember:

Falls at the end of the trail along Corney Brook, Nova Scotia.

#1: KEEP IT SIMPLE

The goal of this approach is to minimize equipment and maximize your freedom to enjoy the sport of fly fishing. You can always go back to more equipment if you want to in the future. For now, pare down and travel light.

#2: VALUE ALL FISH

All fish are beautiful and fascinating in their own way. We can enjoy them all without falling into the trap of becoming "fish snobs." If you can still become as excited by catching a really nice bluegill as a large bass or trout, then you have the right attitude to allow you to enjoy backpack fly fishing.

#3: LOOK AROUND YOU AND NOTICE THE CONNECTIONS OF NATURE

Fish live in the natural environment with all its intricate interconnections of geography, weather, bird life, and wildlife. Becoming more attuned to these connections not only helps us appreciate nature more but makes us better flyfishers.

#4: PERSONALIZE YOUR FLY SELECTIONS AND EQUIPMENT

The backpack fly-fishing approach is simple, but it is up to each flyfisher to personalize his or her fly selection and fly rod choice to fit the local area. This is a never-ending process that will be shaped over time by one's own personal experiences, successes, failures, and memorable times.

A stand of red pines along Tobyhanna Creek, Pennsylvania.

#5: "BLUR" THE LINE BETWEEN FISHING AND OTHER OUTDOOR ACTIVITIES

When in doubt, bring your backpack, whether or not you intend on fishing. You will be surprised how many opportunities for fishing arise when you are doing something else. The key is to think of your backpack as something that you always bring with you, just in case.

#6: KEEP ACCURATE RECORDS

Fishing journals are a fun and useful way to track your own fly-fishing history. Recording your catches reinforces your successes and creates a personal database of what fish you have caught, how big they were, and when, where, and how you caught them.

#7: FISH WITH PEOPLE WHO DO AND DON'T FISH

Because all we have to do is carry a backpack, we can engage in backpack fly fishing with all kinds of people. We are not restricted to fishing with other people who fish and, as long as our companions are tolerant of our occasional pauses on a hike to take a few casts, we will have plenty of time and opportunities to fish.

#8: USE YOUR CREATIVITY

This point is particularly true with tying flies, but it is also related to our decisions about where and when to pursue fish. Some of the most satisfying fish to catch are those that we find by using deductive reasoning to locate. It is incredibly gratifying to puzzle out where fish may be found based on our knowledge of their habits, habitats, and preferred foods.

#9: ACCEPT YOUR MISTAKES AND LEARN FROM THEM

Every activity that we engage in becomes easier once we can identify our mistakes and learn from them. As in all things, we try not to make the same mistakes again and again, even though we probably will a few times before we correct them. We learn through our experiences as we implement the five steps of the ASCAL process, because, as discussed in chapter 2, each of the steps (approach, select a fly, cast, animate the fly, and land the fish) are open to numerous potential errors. It is not easy to get it right!

Sand Spring Run in Hickory Run State Park, Pennsylvania.

#10: FISH CLOSE TO HOME AND FARTHER AWAY

The backpack fly-fishing approach can be used anywhere, and our range of possible places to fish will expand with our experience. It is helpful to think in terms of concentric circles for places within a half hour of your home, within an hour, or further out. Also, we can keep track of information and brochures about places farther afield that we may only visit once every several years on a longer trip.

#11: DO AS MUCH OR AS LITTLE AS YOU LIKE

Recently, I compared a young flyfisherman and, on a separate occasion, an older gentleman. Although the older man could not handle the more strenuous hiking of the younger man, he could wade in the shallows of a lake and take some casts. It reminded me that, in backpack fly fishing, we can take it easy or we can connect our fishing to long and strenuous hikes—it really is up to us how much we want to do. This is a great lifelong hobby precisely because it lends itself to both older and younger people, and to people with less or more mobility.

#12: IT ALL COMES DOWN TO ONE FLY AND ONE FISH

Finally, regardless of equipment, it all comes down to one fly and a flyfisher trying to make a fish go after it. This is and will always be the essence of fly fishing, and it is one of the overriding reasons that I enjoy this approach to fly fishing, because we can enjoy the sport unencumbered by an overabundance of equipment. We just take the handful of flies in which we have the most confidence, tie on the one that we think has the best chance, and cast!

Appendix:

Accessibility and Access for People with Disabilities

I have been involved in the field of special education and rehabilitation for people with disabilities for over forty years. One of the most important things that I have learned during that time is that *all of us* will experience some type of disability during our lifetime, particularly if we live to an older age. If we live long enough, we will experience decreasing mobility, more aches and pains, poorer hearing or vision, poorer balance, and so forth. When I had my hip replaced due to severe osteoarthritis a few years ago, I had to resume my fly fishing from an accessible dock in a local conservation center—with my backpack, fly rod, and cane. Those few small bluegills were terrific fun and helped encourage my continued rehabilitation.

That experience reinforced the idea for me that we *all* need to be concerned about accessibility of beautiful out-

Fly fishing from an accessible fishing pier.

door places for people who experience more challenges than we might. Increasingly, people with disabilities are challenging the assumptions of what is possible for them, and our society has become more accessible. We as a society have realized that increased accessibility benefits *all* people, not just people with disabilities (a concept referred to as *universal design*). For these reasons, we should welcome efforts to create access to lakes, trails, rivers, and streams for people with disabilities, because we will all benefit from them.

So, when you go to your favorite places to hike or fish, note how accessible the facilities are. Is there an accessible dock from which people in wheelchairs could cast, and are the railings low enough to allow casting while ensuring safety? Are campground washrooms accessible to people with different disabilities? Are trails and board-walks usable by people with limited mobility? Keep these questions in mind, and you will become more attuned to greater universal access to the great outdoors for all citizens.

Acknowledgments

I want to thank a number of people who have shaped and influenced the development of the philosophy and practice of backpack fly fishing.

First, I want to thank great friends who have been fishing companions at one time or another: Tom Oliver, Rhey Plumley, Alan Davis, Ernie Pancsofar, John Butterworth, Tony Hecimovic, and Tom Powell. I have had great times with all of them and learned a lot along the way.

The fine professionals who maintain the national, provincial, and state parks in the United States and Canada deserve particular recognition. We are incredibly fortunate that these varied park systems and the fish and wildlife within them are available to us. Without the hard work and dedication of the staff of these parks, the quality and scope of these resources would not be available.

I also want to thank the Skyhorse Publishing team for taking a chance on this book and for their highly professional support and guidance in its writing and completion. Particular thanks go to Lindsey Breuer for doing such a terrific job in providing the support and encouragement that I needed in completing the book.

I want to thank friends and family who have endured my long lectures and treatises on the topic of the backpack fly-fishing approach and have supported me throughout.

Thanks to my brother Dave and sister Jane, to my sons Zach and Brendan, and to my friends Margaret and Tom Oliver for their support and encouragement as I worked my way through this project. Particular thanks to Margaret Oliver for suggesting the term "simplifly" for this book. Sincere thanks go to the entire Rivara family for allowing me to fish on their farm pond.

Thanks to Kathy Steere, Matt Oliver, and Tom Oliver for their help in proofreading and/or providing feedback on earlier drafts of this book. Their input was instrumental in helping to improve the quality of the book.

Zach and Kathy did a phenomenal job with the principal photography, which added so much to the book's quality. My sincere thanks to both of them for doing such an excellent job.

As always, my particular thanks go to my wife, Kathy, for being my most constant companion and supporter throughout all of my strange endeavors, including the development of this book. She is so many things to me, not the least of which is a great fishing companion.

And a final note of thanks and particular recognition goes to my friend and fishing partner Tom Oliver, who taught me how to fish and whose stories of past fishing exploits, told over a few too many beers in a cramped New Jersey shore town apartment one hot night, got it all started.

For Further Reading

There are so many excellent books and other resources available on the topics of fly fishing and fly tying, and I have benefitted from reading many of them. However, as I think back on what drew me to backpack fly fishing, a few stand out.

BOOKS

Universal Fly Tying Guide by Dick Stewart (Stephen Greene Press, 1979, updated in 1994; Alan C. Hood & Company reprint in 2007).

This was my first book on fly tying and it really got me into the different types of flies. The photographs are beautiful and the tying descriptions are clear. I find that I refer back to it again and again to get excited about fly fishing and fly tying.

LL Bean Fly Fishing for Bass Handbook by Dave Whitlock (Lyons Press, 1988, updated in 2000 and 2007).

It was the introduction to this book that first caught my attention, because the author pointed out that, to a large degree, flyfishers have associated fly fishing primarily with coldwater fish (trout and salmon) and have ignored the opportunities of warmwater fishing. This book, plus the author's later series of articles on fly fishing for panfish in *Fly Fisherman* magazine, had a big effect on my thinking about how and when to fly fish.

Fly Fishing Small Streams by John Gierach (Stackpole Books, 1989).
Although he has written so many excellent books, this one had the greatest impact on me because it captured the idea of fishing small streams with less equipment.

Bass Flies by Dick Stewart (Northland Press, 1989).
This beautifully illustrated book extended my knowledge of tying flies for warmwater fish. It is a tremendously helpful instructional guide to tying a range of flies for bass and panfish.

The Art of Fly Tying by Claude Chartrand (Firefly Books, 1999).
Translated from the original French, this beautifully photographed and comprehensive guide to fly tying is a wonderful addition to one's fly-tying library. In particular, I enjoy reading the histories of different flies, and the author introduced me to flies that I had not encountered and that have been effective. The Chief Needahbeh, a colorful and effective streamer, was new to me, and I have tied and used it with success, particularly for bass.

The Simon and Schuster Pocket Guide to Trout and Salmon Flies by John Buckland (Simon & Schuster, 1986).
This guide to flies, published in Great Britain, is truly international, with flies organized by shape and color. It

is fascinating to compare flies from countries across the globe. This book was purchased as a gift for me by my parents in Charlottetown, Prince Edward Island.

Bluegill Fly Fishing & Flies by Terry and Roxanne Wilson (Frank Amato Publications, 1999).

This book is extremely valuable in helping to extend your skills on fishing for bluegills. If nothing else, the Bully's Bluegill Spider has been a tremendous fly for me, and it is available nowhere around here. I strongly suggest that you buy the book and then tie several of the Bully's Bluegill Spiders for your fly box!

Bass Bug Fishing by William G. Tapply (The Lyons Press, 1999).

I love all of Tapply's writing, both about the outdoors and his mystery stories. This book reminds us to keep it simple and fish for bass in the most fun way, on top!

Stripers and Streamers by Ray Bondorew (Frank Amato Publications, 1996).

Although I hail from Rhode Island, I did not fly fish for stripers and other saltwater fish until 1999. This terrific book, written by a fellow Rhode Islander, was an invaluable guide.

The Game Fishes of New England and Southeastern Canada by Peter Thompson (Down East Publications, 1980).

I picked up this book in a sale bin in 1984 and it has been invaluable ever since. Thompson's descriptions and wonderful illustrations of both saltwater and freshwater fish are fascinating and extremely useful, particularly for identification of features of different fish. I have not seen this book elsewhere, and it is a shame, for it is one of my favorites.

The Bantam Great Outdoors Guide to the United States and Canada: The Complete Travel Encyclopedia and Wilderness Guide by Val Landi (Bantam Books, 1978).

Although this book is dated and out of print, I have to mention it because it inspired us to investigate Cape Breton Highlands National Park. I am still on the lookout for such a comprehensive guide to outdoor recreation in all fifty states and all of the Canadian provinces.

Pennsylvania Fishes (Pennsylvania Fish & Boat Commission, 2000).

This publication, prepared by the staff of the Pennsylvania Fish & Boat Commission, is an excellent resource in helping to identify the characteristics, life cycle, and habits of different fish. The illustrations are accurate and extremely helpful in fish identification. Your state fish management agency undoubtedly has issued a similar publication, and I urge you to obtain a copy.

Pennsylvania Trout and Salmon Fishing Guide by Mike Sajna (Frank Amato Publications, 1988).
Trout Streams of Pennsylvania by Dwight Landis (Hempstead-Lyndell, 1991 updated 2000).

These two guides for places to fish for trout in my home state have proven useful to me over the past twenty years. I particularly like Sajna's book, because it also includes history related to each location, which adds a lot of interest for me. I suggest that you seek out similar guides for places to fish in your own state or province.

Favorite Flies and Their Histories by Mary Orvis Marbury (Skyhorse Publishing, 2013).

This book was first published in 1892 by the daughter of Charles Orvis, the founder of the Orvis company. It is a fascinating look into flies of the past.

Pennsylvania Atlas and Gazetteer (DeLorme Mapping Co., P.O. Box 298, Freeport, Maine, 04032, 1990, recent edition 2012).

This company publishes detailed atlases for each of the fifty states. These are very helpful in finding small bodies of water and the roads that might lead to them.

BROCHURES OF NATIONAL AND STATE PARKS

National and state parks publish brochures and park maps both in hard copy and on their websites, and I have found these to be extremely valuable in determining where to hike, camp, and fish. For this book, I have consulted brochures and maps for the following state, national, and provincial parks:

- Cape Breton Highlands National Park (Canada)

- Hickory Run State Park (PA)
- Little Pine State Park (PA)
- Shenandoah National Park (VA)
- Tobyhanna and Gouldsboro State Parks (PA)
- Yellowstone National Park (WY)

Again, you should refer to the maps and brochures of those parks that you visit or frequent, because they will provide you with a wealth of information about places to fish, the histories of the areas, and wildlife that you might encounter.

Photo Credits

Introduction
Pages ix, xiv: Zach Steere

Chapter 1
Pages 2, 3: Zach Steere
Pages 4, 8, 11, 12: Kathy Steere

Chapter 2
Pages 16, 19, 21, 24: Zach Steere
Pages 18, 22: Kathy Steere
Page 25: Daniel E. Steere

Chapter 3
Pages 32, 33, 36, 38, 39, 40, 56: Daniel E. Steere
Pages 35, 37, 43, 46, 53, 57, 58: Kathy Steere
Pages 41, 42, 54: Zach Steere

Chapter 4
Pages 61, 62, 64, 81: Daniel E. Steere
Pages 77, 78, 79: Kathy Steere

Chapter 5
Pages 85, 89, 90, 91, 94, 95, 96, 97, 99, 100, 101, 102, 106, 108, 134: Zach Steere

Pages 92, 93, 104, 109, 112, 119, 120, 121, 122, 123, 124, 125, 126, 129: Kathy Steere
Pages 114, 118, 137: Daniel E. Steere

Chapter 6
Pages 143, 163: Daniel E. Steere
Pages 153, 155, 156: Zach Steere
Pages146, 159: Kathy Steere

Afterward
Pages167, 169, 171: Zach Steere

Appendix
Page 174: Kathy Steere

NOTES

NOTES

NOTES

NOTES

NOTES

NOTES